EXCUSE ME,
YOUR LIFE IS
NOW

EXCUSE ME, YOUR LIFE IS NOW

Mastering the Law of Attraction

DOREEN BANASZAK

HAMPTON ROADS
PUBLISHING COMPANY, INC.

Cover design by Jane Hagaman

Hampton Roads Publishing Company, Inc.
1125 Stoney Ridge Road
Charlottesville, VA 22902

434-296-2772
fax: 434-296-5096
e-mail: hrpc@hrpub.com
www.hrpub.com

If you are unable to order this book from your local
bookseller, you may order directly from the publisher.
Call 1-800-766-8009, toll-free.

Library of Congress Cataloging-in-Publication Data

Banaszak, Doreen, 1965-
  Excuse me, your life is now : mastering the law of attraction / Doreen Banaszak.
    p. cm.
  Summary: "Lynn Grabhorn's wildly popular book, *Excuse Me, Your Life Is
Waiting*, offered four fundamental principles for attracting what we desire
most in life. Now Doreen Banaszak has created a sequel that not only presents
a convenient review of Grabhorn's four basic tenets but also offers overwhelm-
ing evidence--from an assembled collection of personal accounts--that these
principles really work"--Provided by publisher.
  ISBN 978-1-57174-543-9 (5.5 x 8.5 tp : alk. paper)
  1. Grabhorn, Lynn, 1931- Excuse me, your life is waiting. 2. Spiritual life--
Miscellanea. 3. Expectation (Psychology) 4. Self-fulfilling prophecy. I. Title.
  BF1999.B3748145 2007
  131--dc22
                                          2007014743

ISBN 978-1-57174-543-9
10 9 8 7 6 5 4 3 2
Printed on acid-free paper in Canada

To Lisa,

And, of course,

To Lynn

But the fuller nature desires to be an agent, to create, and not merely to look on: strong love hungers bless, and not merely to behold blessing. And while there is warmth enough in the sun to feed an energetic life, there will still be men to feel "I am lord of this moment's change, and will change it with my soul."

—George Eliot, from *Daniel Deronda*

Contents

Introduction

"I can already start feeling deep changes in my life."

"My life has been changing so much and so wonderfully."

"It was a book that changed my life."

"I recommend it to everyone I know."

"It opened up a whole new world for me."

"I have read it over and over again!"

These were comments I heard as I started talking to people about their experiences with *Excuse Me, Your Life Is Waiting*. How did one simple book have the power to change people's lives so dramatically? Why do so many people feel this book was responsible for changing their lives on such a profound level? And, on a selfish note, how could I possibly write a sequel that would be worthy of such adoration?

I knew Lynn Grabhorn's book was a *New York Times* bestseller, selling over half a million copies (18 thousand out of her garage!), but I didn't know the extent to which her interpretation of the creation principles had impacted her readers.

The magic soon became clear. Lynn gave us hope that there was another way to live our lives that didn't include "settling." She opened up a door through which we could see the life we really wanted, and then she gave us four simple steps to create it. Those four simple steps and the way she presented them have inspired thousands of people to become aware of how they were choosing to be victims and to start being the creators they always were!

The more I talked with people about *Excuse Me, Your Life Is Waiting*, the more I found that they were applying these principles and getting amazing results. Yet they also had a lot of questions. For instance, "How do I do this consistently?" What had started as an assignment to write an inspirational follow-up was clearly becoming an opportunity to take Lynn's work and her readers to the next level.

Lynn opened the door; I am now taking the opportunity to push you over the threshold by showing you that your life is NOW, not off in the future. In actuality, you are already living it—you just aren't *experiencing* it the way you really want! Lynn woke you up; I'm going to teach you how to *stay* awake.

Have you felt the desire to be more conscious lately? Well, now's your chance. In *Excuse Me, Your Life Is Waiting*, Lynn Grabhorn gave us the manual for waking up to our power to create our reality. In this book, you'll find some real-life examples of people who applied Lynn's principles, found their own power, and changed their lives. You'll also find ways to take your understanding of your power to the next level. This is a "how-to" book with a twist—*you* create the "how-to." That's because only you are the expert in your own experience.

So start by asking yourself, "Why am I reading this book?" Maybe you're a fan of Lynn Grabhorn's book, *Excuse Me, Your Life Is Waiting*, and want to learn more about the Law of Attraction. Or maybe you don't know anything about Lynn's work, but you saw this book on the shelf and it looked interesting. Perhaps you're acquainted with me and/or my work. Maybe you were attracted to the title. It is pretty cool, isn't it? Maybe the book fell off the shelf just as you were passing by. Is it important to know why you chose this book? You bet it is, because whether you are conscious of it or not, you attracted this book into your experience. There is a reason you are reading it—a reason only you know!

You've heard it before: there are no coincidences. That's because you are the sole creator of your experience. It is my intention to teach you how to get conscious and stay awake to the fact that you can live consciously.

So why are you reading this? If you don't know now, I bet you will by the end of this book!

ONE

What Are Creation Principles?

To every one of us who finally ... maybe ...
possibly ... believes they have the right to
perpetual happiness, beginning now.
—Lynn Grabhorn, *Excuse Me, Your Life Is
Waiting,* from the dedication

Congratulations! Your willingness to read this book means that you do believe that you have the right to perpetual happiness. The steps presented in the next few pages will give you the tools to create your happiness, "beginning now." I've started with Lynn's dedication because I think it is one of the best ever written, and it sets the tone for what she and I want for you—to create your life the way you want to, not how you think you "should."

Lynn's central ideas are summarized below, along with a few little exercises to get you in the deliberate creation groove. For those of you who have read *Excuse Me, Your Life Is Waiting,* this review will be a great chance to brush up a bit on the principles in preparation for you to learn how to apply them consistently in your daily life. If you haven't read *Excuse Me, Your Life Is*

Waiting, I encourage you to, as Lynn's explanations will help you to get a better handle on the concepts throughout this book. But even if you don't read Lynn's book first, I'm confident that the words in this book are going to change your life in ways you could never have imagined!

The Four Steps of the Law of Deliberate Creation

So let's get started. There are only four steps to deliberately creating anything you want. They are:

1. Know what you DON'T want.
2. Know what you DO want.
3. Get into the feeling place of what you DO want.
4. Allow what you DO want to come into your experience.

Part of this process is a willingness on your part to believe that you are not alone, that you have a partner who helps to take care of all the details of delivering your desire. Some may call this partner the universe, or God, or Higher Self. For the remainder of the book, I will refer to this partner as your creation partner. I will explain more about how to work closely with this partner a little later. Lynn wanted us to be sure we understood that creation is not just a process of *thought;* it is a process propelled and maintained by *feeling.* There's a difference between thoughts and feelings. We can think all we want, but if we don't actually *feel* what it is that we want, we don't vibrate our energy in alignment with our desires, and therefore we aren't using all of our power to attract what we want.

It's kind of like choosing to start a fire with two sticks when you have a lit blowtorch sitting next to you.

It seems nonsensical, but we all do it; we make our experience harder than it has to be by choosing not to use all of the tools at our disposal.

What is the beauty of this? Since everything in our experience is attracted through our feelings, then our power to create is an inside job—we are the only ones who can create our own experience!

If this is true, we are not the *victims* of our circumstances; we are the *creators* of them!

I know, I know, some of you may be thinking that there is no way that you *wanted* to create your current circumstances—and I'm not here to convince you that you are responsible for losing your job, breaking up with your partner, or dropping your favorite ring down the drain. What's done is done, and there's no sense in dwelling on it. Instead, I am inviting you to focus on the here and now, to accept and change your thoughts and feelings about your current circumstances, so that you can accept the freedom that already exists for you— THE ABILITY TO CREATE A NEW EXPERIENCE!

For some people, accepting the belief that we can create our lives, from the little to the big, will not happen overnight. However, if you are open to the possibility of deliberate creation, and you start taking the four steps toward what you really want, you will soon see results that prove you have the innate freedom to create the experience you really want.

Lynn sums it up nicely in her wonderfully direct manner:

We came here with a guaranteed freedom of choice mandated by the very nature of our existence. The time has come for us to exercise that birthright. We are caught in no one's web. We are bound by no circumstance. We are victims to no conditions. Rather, we are beings who possess the sacred ability to implement any outlandish desire our limitless minds can concoct, for we possess unregulated, unrestricted, uncontested freedom of choice, no matter what those choices may be.

Now, doesn't that feel better than "I have no choice"?

So for the rest of this book, be willing to consider the idea that you create your own experience. Spend time thinking about your current circumstances, and start to recognize which thoughts and feelings serve you and which ones don't. Start putting your attention on new thoughts and new feelings that will create your next series of desired circumstances.

Putting the Laws into Action

The Law of Attraction and the Law of Deliberate Creation work hand in hand. The Law of Attraction states that like attracts like. If you put out positive feelings, you'll get back a positive outcome. If you emit negative feelings, you'll get a negative result. How can you make sure you're putting out positive thoughts to attract good things into your life? You do this by practicing the four steps of the Law of Deliberate Creation, which states that you create that upon which you put your attention.

Therefore, if you want to have more money, you have to put your attention on creating positive feelings around the idea of money in order to attract more money into your life. The great thing about these laws is that they are universal. You probably never realized that you are already applying them unconsciously! But when you apply them unconsciously, you have no control over the results. When applied consciously, they give the results you truly desire. There are no exceptions; this concept works equally for everyone. So, let's look at this process in more depth.

Step 1. Know What You DON'T Want

You might think it's odd to start here, especially after what I just said about not focusing on negativity, but here's the thing—a lot of us have a hard time figuring out what we really want. It's much easier to articulate what we *don't* want because we tend to do this naturally anyway. Recently, for example, I've noticed that my three-year-old daughter Samantha will say, "I don't want her playing with my toy!" or "I don't want to do that." I'm not sure where this comes from, as I pay close attention to how we phrase the things we say, but in response, I have been asking her to "tell me what you DO want." In this way, she is turning a "don't want" into a "do want." It's a simple process that you can practice, too. The technique of starting with what we don't want can sometimes jumpstart our thinking toward what we do want.

Having your attention on what you don't want keeps you squarely locked on what you don't want to have happen, and, according to the Law of Attraction, this is what you're most likely to draw into your life! Being fearful about something is the fastest way to bring it into your experience. But by first identifying what you don't want, you can face your fears and then choose to put your attention and energy on that which you do want.

So let's get started. Get out a piece of paper or get on the computer, and write a list of all your "don't wants." For example:

- I don't want to fail.
- I don't want to get sick.
- I don't want my kids to get hurt.

- I don't want to go out of business.
- I don't want to work here anymore.

Now let's move on to Step 2, in which we can use these "don't wants" to help us identify what we really do want. Once we are clearer on what we want, we can focus our attention on those things, rather than the "don't wants" we've been concentrating on up to now.

Step 2. Know What You DO Want

Now that you wrote your list of "don't wants," writing your "do wants" is a piece of cake! Simply rewrite your "don't wants" as "do wants":

- "I don't want to fail" becomes "I want to be successful."
- "I don't want to get sick" becomes "I want perfect health."
- "I don't want my kids to get hurt" becomes "I want my kids to be safe and healthy."
- "I don't want to go out of business" becomes "I want my business to be successful."
- "I don't want to work here anymore" becomes "I want to find work that I love."

That's easy, right? Those are the positive wants, and they should feel pretty good when you say them aloud. Remember, you aren't pining or longing for them, but conjuring and savoring the feelings associated with *having* them.

But beware of getting caught up in the trap of expressing "negative wants." If your "do wants" make you feel badly about yourself, then they're not positive. Like the proverbial wolf in sheep's clothing, they're simply more bad news, but in a nice, fuzzy costume. For example:

- "I want to be thin."
- "I want to be rich."
- "I want to be pain-free."

For the most part, these tend to be focused on what you are not: you are not thin, rich, or pain-free. And focusing on *that* doesn't feel so good. In fact, saying them probably feels like eating a prickly pear.

To counteract negative wants, restate them in a way that feels good. Maybe the following will resonate more for you . . .

- "I want to learn how to eat well."
- "I want to learn how to earn money doing work I love."
- "I want to learn about alternative ways to be healthy."

Note that choosing to learn about something is a great way to be focused on the positive while creating a next step.

Finally, if you're the kind of person who feels guilty about wanting things—that perhaps you're not good enough or deserving of good things in your life—then you need to know about the concept of "rightful wants." Lynn tells us: "With rightful wants, we accept the very real fact that it is not only appropriate and proper, but critical for us to want: anything . . . any-where . . . of any kind . . . in any amount . . . in any shape . . . to any degree . . . at any time we so desire. Anything!" So, get rid of the guilt! You deserve good things in your life just as much as the other guy. Accepting this idea is going to be very important for the next step. Start to really think about and believe in what Lynn is telling you here, as it will make the difference between frustration and success with these principles.

Step 3. Get into the Feeling
Place of What You DO Want

Some people who read *Excuse Me, Your Life Is Waiting* thought that Lynn repeated herself a lot throughout the book, especially when it came to the word FEELINGS. Well, there was good reason for the repetition, because feelings are what this whole process of creation is based on. Unfortunately, we typically rely on our thinking, not our feelings. If you don't *feel* good—no matter what you happen to be thinking—you are creating what you don't want. If you feel good, you are creating what you do want.

It really is that simple!

Of course, thoughts and feelings are connected. Try this: think of something that makes you feel sad . . . Now, while thinking about it, be happy. It simply is not possible to think sad thoughts and feel happy at the same time.

So if you are thinking about a circumstance in your life that you feel badly about, banish those thoughts from your mind because those negative thoughts will never generate the positive feelings you need to change an unwanted circumstance.

Lynn was adamant in her repetition of the importance of feelings because, for most of us, it seems much easier to be stuck in our bad feelings than to shift those feelings in a way that will ultimately change our circumstances. She even suggested that spending at least 16 seconds flowing powerful positive feelings was a great start to bring what we want into our reality. (Many people have asked where the idea of 16 seconds came from, and I honestly don't know, but I'm confident that Lynn knew what she was talking about!) Whether it's 16 seconds or 16 hours, what I do know is that any amount of time you can feel powerful and positive is time well spent!

Okay, so how do you change how you feel? Just do what you've been doing so far:

- You've identified what you don't want.
- You've identified what you do want, and you are feeling good about having it.

Now you want to feel even better about it! Remember that the Law of Attraction means that like attracts like. You want to create such a good feeling about what you desire that you start to attract that desire into your experience. In fact, the better you feel and the more positive attention you put on your want, the faster it will come!

Lynn refers to this as "buzzing," or raising our frequency. Emotional frequencies are just vibrations. In essence, what you are learning to do is to manage your energy vibration by managing your feelings. So get a "buzz on" about your want!

Take one of your wants and ask yourself the following questions:

- What feelings will I have more of when I get this want that I don't have today?
- How will I change when I get this want?
- How will my life change when I get this want?
- What do I see my life looking like when I get this want?

Now, write out a script or vision of this want, a wonderful mini-story. You'll know you have been successful at ramping up your feelings when you read your ministory aloud to yourself and you FEEL the way you've described feeling in your answers to the questions above.

Also, as this is happening, pay attention to the place

in your body where you are feeling your positive energy. Is it in your stomach, your solar plexus, your head? Positive feelings in your body are physical proof that you are creating, not "miss-creating"!

Step 4. Allow What You DO Want to Come into Your Experience

Okay, a quick review . . .

- You've identified what you don't want.
- You've identified what you do want.
- You've gotten your "buzz on" about your want.

Now, the fourth step . . .

What typically happens when we decide what we want? Usually, we start taking a ton of actions to get it. Maybe we write frantic to-do lists, or race around in search of this or that. Lynn called this "Hi-Ho Silvering," and it isn't very effective, because it doesn't feel good! It just makes us feel stressed.

Do keep in mind that I am not recommending that you just sit around and wait for your want. What I mean is that your want will come much faster if you put your attention on allowing it and taking what Lynn called "inspired action." What is inspired action? It's action that is driven by your attention to how you are feeling about the circumstances that present themselves. Here's an example from my own life on how this works.

A few months ago, I had little time and a choice to make. I could do a business task to generate some badly needed new business, or I could do some Web site maintenance. Now, most of you entrepreneurs out there would say this was an easy choice: go after some new business, right? In days gone by, I would have done exactly that, but that day that option just didn't feel good. It felt better, and more inspired, to do the maintenance, so I did. Believe me, I was pretty amazed that I made that choice, too!

First, I put my attention on the maintenance going smoothly, I updated my Web site with some new class dates, and I made the site look better, too. A few hours later, I got an e-mail from someone who had just recommended my Web site to a large list of clients. If I hadn't done the site maintenance, I realized, all of the new people coming to my site would have found outdated information, and I would have lost multiple opportunities for new business.

Did I know that my Web address was going to be sent out? Nope. Did I know that there was another opportunity looming for new business? Nope. All I knew was that I wanted new business and that I felt inspired to update my Web site, so I did, and look at the payoff!

When you are forcing your actions, it doesn't feel good. Not feeling good means that you are not creating in the direction of what you want. In fact, it means that you are creating in the opposite direction! Remember, you engage not only your own power, but also the power of your creation partner when you allow and feel good about the actions you are taking.

What I want you to know is that it is not okay to wait any longer for your life. You were given the power to create any experience you want, and it is as simple as following these four steps:

- Know what you don't want.
- Know what you do want.
- Get your "buzz on" about your want.
- Allow your want to come naturally into your experience.

But to have success with these steps you have to be willing to accept all of your fears, jealousies, thoughts of separateness, anxieties, anger, frustrations, and limiting beliefs. Why? Because when you accept what doesn't feel good, you release that energy and can use it to keep your thoughts and feelings on the positive results that you really want.

The Four Steps in Action: How I Used Them in My Own Life

The best way to demonstrate how to effectively use the four steps to change your life for the better is to give you an example, one that a lot of folks have asked me about—how did I get this gig? How did I apply the process to creating an opportunity to write the follow-up to a *New York Times* bestseller? Well, I started where Lynn told us to start . . .

My "Don't Wants"

Let's start with what I didn't want. I didn't want my life-coaching business to fail. I didn't want to go back to corporate America. I didn't want to market my business in ways that I didn't feel comfortable with. I didn't want to lose my house. I didn't want to live moment to moment financially. I didn't want to live in financial fear. I didn't want to disappoint my partner. Did I mention that I didn't want to fail?

So guess what my reality became? My business was failing. I contemplated going back to corporate America. I was forcing all these marketing techniques that I hated. I was behind on my mortgage payments. Every moment was filled with financial fear. I stopped believing in myself so my partner had no choice but to stop believing in me. I got exactly what I feared. I was failing big time!

So you can see what an amazing job I was doing at creating the life I didn't want! That's what I love about these laws: they don't judge, they just deliver.

Believe me, this is not something I want a bazillion people to know about my life, but it is important to recognize how I was unconsciously attracting the things I didn't want, so that I can demonstrate for you how good we can all become at creating the things we really do want.

So I was feeling pretty badly about myself and about my life, and I continued to get more of the same: bad feelings with bad results. Bottom line, it wasn't getting any better! You know the saying, "when you hit rock bottom, there's no other way but up"? Well, rock bottom was where I was when I finally decided to pick myself up and start rethinking and refeeling what I was doing.

I had read *Excuse Me, Your Life Is Waiting* a couple of years back, had enjoyed it, and had really wanted to apply the creation principles in my life. But, like most people, I read it and then I put it down so I could be sure to keep my attention squarely on what I didn't want. After all, that's what I'd been doing all along, and I was pretty good at it!

This time, though, I picked up the book again and started thinking about what I really wanted for my business, my life, and myself.

My "Do Wants"

In my desperation, I had chosen to listen to all the experts out there who said I couldn't possibly get folks to pay my coaching fees without doing all this other work that I just simply didn't want to do. So my attention wasn't on getting clients; it was on doing lots of marketing that I resented doing. It became clear to me that this was a big part of my problem. I was listening to everyone else because I had lost trust in myself to create the life and the business that I truly wanted.

So I focused on getting clear about my intentions. What did I really want? And it came to me . . .

I wanted to get a book deal to write the follow-up to Lynn Grabhorn's *Excuse Me, Your Life Is Waiting.*

No, I'm kidding . . .

What I really wanted was to find my ideal clients and put myself right in front of them so that they would work with me. That was it. Not too specific, but it felt good! I also decided that I wanted to put myself in front of these folks by implementing marketing strategies that were not only effective, but that I enjoyed doing. Now this REALLY felt good!

I figured that if I put my attention on getting my business off the ground, then all the other areas of my life would start to improve. Let's just say this was false hope on my part, but at least it was a start.

My Feeling Place . . .

I have to admit, even after I started focusing on my "do wants," I still wasn't "buzzing" with joy. Like most people in a similar situation, I wasn't seeing a lot of my much-needed results fast enough. But this time I was determined to put the Law of Deliberate Creation to the test. After all, I didn't have much left to lose! Therefore, I just kept putting one foot in front of the other and tried to envision the ideas, thoughts, people, circumstances, and the money pouring in. More important, I paid attention to the feelings I was having about these things. The more I kept myself focused on good feelings, the more good things started to trickle into my life.

My Allowing Place . . .

Now that I knew what I wanted, and I was feeling a bit better, thoughts and ideas started coming to me. One thought was to do a book group on *Excuse Me.* It wasn't a huge stretch, as I'd done book groups on other books like *Excuse Me* in the past. And since I'd reread it recently, it seemed like a good pick.

Typically, I get permission from the author before I do a book group. However, when I went to Lynn's Web site, I found out that she had died. At that point, I could have just gone ahead with the book group, as I only contact authors to give them a heads-up, not because it's necessary. But for some unexplained reason, I felt inspired to take it one step further and get permission from her publisher.

I shot off an e-mail to Hampton Roads Publishing Company, and then I didn't think about it again. A month or two later, I got an e-mail saying that they had just come across my message. The book group idea was fine, they said, but they were also looking for someone to continue doing seminars on *Excuse Me*. Would I be interested in doing that? It sounded like an interesting proposition to me. We decided to meet up.

At this stage, my life still seemed to be headed in the "don't want" direction. Three days before I jumped into my car—the price of airfare was certainly out of the question—to drive 12 hours to Virginia to meet with the publisher, I was on the phone to all the creditors who had been calling my house for the past several months looking for money that I didn't have. When I got to Virginia, I found out that my mortgage was going into foreclosure. On top of all of this, I knew that my relationship of seven years was in crisis, and I didn't have the strength to do anything about it.

Here I was, in my hotel room, by myself, wondering if I should call an ambulance because I was having what could only be called a panic attack. The irony, which is pretty clear, was that I was here to get permission to use Lynn's material to teach people how to consciously create their experience. Believe me, I felt the irony, too—but one little part of me also felt inspired to just keep going, and that was enough to set me on the right track.

I kept asking myself, "What do you want? What do you want?"

Of course, I wanted permission to use Lynn's materials—that was the reason I was meeting with these folks. Having permission to use her material would put me right in front of my ideal clients, which was also what I wanted. But then, all of a sudden, I thought and then actually blurted out loud, "I want a book deal." Why? I have no idea. Maybe it was because I was in desperate need of money and thought I would walk out of there with a big fat advance. I really don't know why a book deal came to mind—it just did, so I went with it.

I spent the morning before the meeting thinking about what I wanted and trying to get myself to the feeling place of having permission to use the materials, working with my ideal clients, and being offered a book deal. Let's just say, it's not the easiest thing to have happy vibrations when you are in the middle of a panic attack, but I did the best I could.

On top of all this, I was feeling a bit like a fraud. Let's not forget, I was about to go into a meeting with practically the entire staff of Hampton Roads to prove to them that I was the best candidate to continue to pass on and teach Lynn's principles of creation when here I was still struggling with them in my own life.

Still, I felt inspired to keep going. I had a feeling of clear guidance. You know how sometimes when things seem chaotic, you feel a strange sense of calm, as if something is taking care of you and guiding you even though you feel completely incapable? It was as if something took over for me, and I was just sitting back and watching me. Now that I knew that I was allowing what I wanted to happen, I decided I'd better get my negative thoughts and feelings out of the way and just allow myself to be guided.

So here I was in this meeting, and it was as if I were

a totally different person from the one in my hotel room. There was no panic, just that wonderful sense of calm. During the meeting, I realized that everything I had chosen for myself in my business was coming together. There had been plenty of stuff over the years that I had enjoyed, but I had been focusing only on the stuff I didn't enjoy. And in that moment I understood that it was all part of my creation.

As I was answering the group's questions, Jack, the CEO of Hampton Roads, turned to me and said, "We've been thinking about writing a follow-up book to *Excuse Me, Your Life Is Waiting.* It would be mostly inspirational stories about how the principles have transformed people's lives. Would you be interested in writing it?"

In my mind's eye, I saw myself falling off my chair. Even though I'd said I wanted a book deal, I certainly didn't expect to get one!

Now this was a very important moment. I had a choice.

I could choose to think that I was not qualified for this. I had never written a book, and I'd heard it's a terribly difficult thing to do. My life was a mess, and I was completely unclear about my future. Would I be a fraud if I took this on? How could I possibly be the one to take these principles and teach them to others, let alone write a book about them?

Or, I could say yes and figure it all out later.

A voice in my head said, "Just say YES." And so I did. Was it my voice? Maybe it was Lynn's. It didn't matter. I simply chose to put all the negative thoughts about myself aside and listen.

It would have been very easy for me to duck out with the excuse that my life was such a mess that I didn't deserve the opportunity and walk away. I could have said something to the tune of, "Excuse me, my *mess* is waiting." Believe me, I had done this in the past on many occasions! I realized only later that I was actually the best person to continue teaching these principles because when I said yes, I was applying them full-on, focusing on what I wanted and allowing it to come into my experience. I was a life-size demonstration that this stuff REALLY WORKS.

So here I sit writing what is, in essence, a long-winded letter to you, inviting you to do as I did . . . to see beyond your circumstances and to think, speak, and act as you truly are, to feel yourself becoming what you want to be.

This book is full of inspirational stories and, just as important, some true lessons learned from the application of the principles in *Excuse Me, Your Life Is Waiting*. It is my intention that you walk away from this experience with the tools to take Lynn's materials to the next level, and also with a deeper understanding of who you really are and what you are really capable of.

TWO

Your Invitation to Get Conscious . . . NOW!

> You never again have to believe that circum-
> stances outside you control your life.
>
> —Lynn Grabhorn,
> *Excuse Me, Your Life Is Waiting*

People ask me the same question all the time: "How do I get off what feels like the roller coaster of my life and start to apply these principles consistently?"

If you saw the 1989 movie *Parenthood,* you'll remember a scene where Steve Martin, who played the father, was at his wit's end chasing his kids around. His face was twisted, his stomach was grumbling, and he was breaking out in a sweat. He looked like he was about to vomit. He yelled to his wife that he hated the roller coaster of his life, and his wife replied, "Well, I love it!" Later in the movie, he learned to love it, too!

Lynn helped us to realize that we are all on some kind of roller-coaster ride of our own creation, whether we realize it or not. This ride has only two types of pas-sengers: those who learn to love it and those who don't. It's not possible to get off the ride, only to gain the inspiration and the tools to consciously create and love—not fear—all of the inevitable bumps, dips, and turns.

As we go through this process together, I invite you not only to read, but to turn all of your inspiration into action. The best way I can help you to do that is to take one of your unfulfilled intentions and put it (and you) through the creation process. By doing this, you will be able to see where you may be encountering "creation frustration," the main cause of inconsistent creation results. But before we get to that, I invite you to start raising your consciousness . . .

We've been given the steps, and they seem simple enough: know what you don't want, know what you do want, feel it, and then allow it. We've tried them. We've had some success, but not consistent success. What is consistent success, you may be wondering, and how do we know when we're getting consistent results? In fact, you may be wondering whether anyone ever really gets those kinds of results.

Remember the Steve Martin character . . . he was on the roller coaster, conscious of the fact that he was hating it. It wasn't until he accepted that he was on the roller coaster—and *chose* to enjoy it—that he actually did.

A lot of us don't even realize that we are on this wonderful ride. We simply go through our days filled with "have-to's," "shoulds," and worse, "don't want to's." Our attention is focused squarely on our doubts, fears, and worries. We are, in essence, unconscious of the fact that we are on the ride of our lives! We are missing the joy of it because we are choosing to experience it as passengers, not as creators.

Why do you think this book is titled *Excuse Me, Your Life Is NOW*? It's because your life does not begin when you get the Ferrari, or the unbelievable partner, or the job of your dreams. Remember the Law of Attraction: like attracts like. If you think your life will get better when you have all the things that you are longing for, then you will just get more longing, more "life will get better later."

The beauty of becoming conscious that you are the creator of your life is that when you do, you will start to realize that life is pretty great as it is right now—and that will start to attract more "great"! So, to answer the question about whether anyone really does have consistent success with these principles, the answer is a resounding "yes!"

In the original *Excuse Me,* Lynn gave us the tools to consciously enjoy our personal roller-coaster ride. If you want fewer bumps, create fewer. If you love the dips, create more dips. The only caveat is that you have to be willing to be conscious full-time, not part-time— or else you will hit the unexpected, unwanted bumps and dips that you fear!

A man named Kim wrote a story about the way he unconsciously created a bumpy ride for himself:

Everything started one day at work. My wife called to say there was a big sale on Kia vans in a town nearby called Omak. She'd wanted a van for a long time, and she talked me into meeting her at the dealership in Omak after work. The whole time I was driving down there, I thought about how I wanted my wife to have the van, but also about how I knew we couldn't really afford the payments. When I got to the lot, she picked the van she wanted, and we bought it anyway.

Time passed, and I hated that monthly payment. It just seemed to cause problems when we most wanted to be able to do other things. I liked the van; I just wasn't happy to have the burden. For months, I stewed. Then one day, as I was driving my wife and daughter to visit my uncle, we had to take a left on a busy street. I remember seeing a motorcycle and a couple of cars coming, so instead of taking the chance to go ahead and turn, I decided to wait. My wife and I were chatting about what we were going to do in town. The next thing I remember, my wife and daughter were screaming. We'd been rear-ended by a teenage boy who'd dropped his cell phone and leaned down to pick it up. He'd hit us at about 55 to 60 miles per hour, and totaled the van.

Well, after I made sure that my family was okay, I jumped out of the van and headed back to yell at the driver, but I saw he was just a teenage boy standing there in shock. He kept telling me he was really sorry, so I asked him if he was okay and we shook hands. We dialed 911, and the police and ambulance showed up.

Now, looking back, I wasn't glad about the accident, of course, but now that I don't have the van payment, it makes everything a lot better with my family and me. My wife, son, and I all have cars that are paid for now—of course, they may not be new, but they are ours. I feel a lot better.

In the end, Kim got what he wanted in the first place: he wanted out of that van payment. The universe gave him a big bump, so to speak, and granted his wish. In fact, if you think about it, doesn't it always seem like in the end we always get what we really wanted in the first place? That's because these principles always deliver what we want, whether we are conscious of it or not!

Kim was unconscious of what he really wanted. If he had simply been honest and applied the creation principles—if he had listened to his Higher Self telling him not to buy the van—he would have saved himself and his family a lot of grief. He could have enjoyed the ride, not been almost thrown off!

People have asked me, "Will my life have fewer negative experiences when I start getting conscious about creating?" The answer is, "If that is what you choose for yourself, of course!" The more conscious you get, the more in sync you are with your creation partner and yourself. And the more in sync, the more enjoyable the ride!

Keep in mind, this ride never stops, and it never slows down; you are on it for good. The minute you start being conscious of your experience of this ride, you become a "conscious creator," consistently getting the results you consciously choose!

So, if consciousness equals consistency, the goal is to wake up and stay awake!

Trust me, I know how hard it may seem, even for someone who is already on the path to becoming a conscious creator. I may have consciously created an incredible opportunity to work with my ideal clients via a book deal, but I certainly didn't come home to a pile of miraculously paid-off bills, a thriving business, and a bank account bursting at the seams. No, I was still feeling badly about myself, and I still had a lot of fear, worry, and doubt. I went back to my unconscious life, and I became an unconscious passenger again.

We all do this sometimes, for many different reasons, but one reason—the one that most profoundly erodes our ability to consistently apply these principles—is that we deny our role in creating our present circumstances. We think it was all just a fluke, or that "something greater than me" made it happen.

When you discredit your role in your creation— knowing what you want, feeling it, and allowing it— you are bound to hit more of those unwanted bumps and dips.

Remember, there are no victims. You are always creating—you are either choosing to do it consciously or unconsciously. There is no in-between!

Many readers of *Excuse Me* will tell you that they have read it multiple times over many years. They will also tell you that no matter how many times they've read it, they always find something new and useful at each successive reading. Why? Because they are raising their consciousness about who they are, what they want, and how to effectively use the principles to create a life aligned with their true selves.

So what is the first step in becoming a conscious creator and staying one?

Understand You Are Not Alone

Lynn says it beautifully . . .

We each came with a partner, this profoundly loving, exclusive chaperone whom we have, by and large, chosen to ignore. Call it Inner Being, Higher Self, Expanded Self, God Self, or Mickey Mouse; call it what you will, it's that greater part of us we're attached to that comes with the physical package. We can't be physical without it, for it's the source that keeps us alive (not living, perhaps, but alive). It is the pure positive energy of Life, which we are.

Imagine that on your roller-coaster ride, you're sitting next to this partner. This partner is your key to the unseen, where all of what comes into your reality is waiting to come in. This partner is really like the magic genie in the bottle because it exists to give you the experiences you command.

You communicate with this partner through your thoughts and feelings. The only way your partner can work with you is through the Law of Attraction. You have free will, so your partner doesn't judge what you are requesting through your thoughts and feelings; it just delivers!

But if we do have such power, and a helpful partner to boot, why have many folks written that they have taken the steps, but they still aren't getting what they want? We will get into more of the reasons for this as we go through this book, but at a primary level, if we don't understand our role in this partnership, then we won't have our conscious attention where it needs to be to create what we choose to experience.

Now Lynn gave us the four-step creation process:

• Know what you don't want.
• Know what you do want.
• Get into the feeling place of what you want.
• Allow it to come into your experience.

So our job is also to . . .

• Get clear.
• Stay clear.

. . . and then the hardest:

• Get out of your creation partner's way.

Once you are clear about what you want, you are already communicating that desire to your partner through your thoughts and feelings. As you think about what you want, and feel how it will be to have it, you are vibrating your desire and making it even more clear to your partner. If you start to doubt, then you begin sending mixed signals. Remember, your creation partner only goes by the Law of Attraction, so sending out mixed signals means attracting them, too.

Keeping your attention on your original intention is your job! Once you consistently do this, then you need to get out of your partner's way. Your partner's job is to make the "how" happen. The more you get out of your partner's way when it comes to the mechanism that will effect change, the more you allow your desires into your life!

It is easy to start asking yourself, "But how can I make this happen?" It is what we have always done, but if you want to be a conscious creator, you will have to be willing to stick to your job and let your partner do so as well! In order to be a conscious creator, you must be willing to stay conscious of your partnership and your role in it. If you lose sight of this, you will slow down, manifest at a snail's pace, and give yourself some more of those unwanted bumps!

What will block your communication with your creation partner? Fear, doubt, and worry! How do you manage these? Start by creating new beliefs.

Create New Beliefs!

"Change my beliefs? Isn't that harder than just creating something I want?"

Three things: first, I didn't say, "change"; I said "create." There's a difference. Second, from this point forward, be consistently conscious of the fact that what you think about and feel, you will create! If you think creating new beliefs is hard, you're right, it will be. If you think creating new beliefs is easy, you're right, it will be! Third, the process of creation is always the same, whether you use it to create a million dollars, or a new belief, or even a new you. (Pssst: that's what you are really doing, by the way!)

The goal is to create new, positive, powerful beliefs. They don't need to override the old ones, just to become the ones you pay attention to the most.

Why is this so important? Because becoming a conscious creator with consistent results is a full-time job. Spending 16 seconds on an intention is great, but if you want significant and consistent results, this process of creation has to become your conscious nature, and your conscious nature is managed by your beliefs. In other words, scripting and visualizing a million dollars in your experience is great and will generate results, but only if you don't spend the rest of your day feeling badly that there's never enough money to go around. How could your creation partner possibly deliver your million dollars if you believe there isn't enough money to go around?

Lynn wrote that we were "taught backwards." Most of us were taught that:

- Life is a series of circumstances.
- We have to labor in order to have.
- It is best to be cautious.

Why? We were fine until we started getting socialized, until we accepted other people's truths and started hiding our own. Who are those other people? They're the ones who told me I was showing off when I was so excited to get up on water skis on my first try. The ones who told me that my batting stance and one-handed lay-up were all wrong, even though I excelled in both hitting and baskets scored. They're the ones who leered at me when I clapped after a church sermon because I was so excited by it.

I admit that I let those other people wear me down. I chose to hide my truth and who I really was, and I started believing their truths instead. When we live by these, we are literally living our lives according to what we don't want!

The principles of deliberate creation are designed to help us change this tide, to flip "don't wants" into "do wants":

- Life is a series of events that I have consciously created.
- Everything I want comes to me naturally and effortlessly.
- Freedom is in surrender.
- My life is always focused on what I want.

I invite you to create some new beliefs, too—not just to reverse a few of your old and un-useful beliefs—about how life really works and your role in it.

Also, I invite you to consider adopting the following seven Creation Foundation Beliefs based on your new understanding of your partnership:

1. I appreciate that my truth is my truth.
2. I am not my current circumstance; I am its creator.
3. I am connected to my creation partner through my thoughts and feelings.
4. My creation partner wants and provides all I choose for myself without fail.
5. I have complete free will, and I know that nothing can be done *to* me; it has to come *through* me.
6. I can be, do, or have anything.
7. Everything is unfolding perfectly for me now.

Please note that I am not here to convince you of anything—your truth is your truth. I invite you not to analyze these new beliefs, but to try them out in your experience to see if they feel good and right to you. I invite you to accept them as a child would accept a lesson from a teacher. Why not? You have nothing to lose and so much more to gain by experiencing them for yourself.

Let's break these down, one by one . . .

I Appreciate That My Truth Is My Truth

How do you know if something is true or not? There are so many people and institutions out there saying various and sometimes conflicting things; how do we *know* what truth really is? It's simple: you decide. Take all of the information, filter it down, cast out what you don't believe, and adopt what you believe. How do you know what your truth is? It FEELS good!

What you believe will, in turn, shape and contour your personal experience of the world. Since you decide what the truth is, your truth *is* the truth for you!

Most of you can probably get behind that one, but now how about when it comes to speaking your truth in all circumstances?

In response, the first thing people usually say is, "That is so selfish." But is it really? Kim chose to buy the van when his truth was that they couldn't afford it. What happened after Kim bought the van? He resented making the payments, and then consequently resented his wife for talking him into it, which caused stress in their relationship, which caused discomfort among their children, which caused . . .

Now what if Kim had been honest? At the most, he would have avoided some of the stress above. At the least, he would have felt validated because he spoke his truth and didn't bury it. Even if his wife didn't agree and they bought the van, Kim would have spoken his truth and been able to deal with his feeling about the van more clearly. Because he chose to bury his truth, he created stress within his family, the effect of which was an accident that could have been much worse than it was.

So what is more selfish really—speaking your truth, or burying it?

Your truth is who you are. Your truth is your consciousness screaming for recognition. Burying it only causes harm to you and those around you. Can you think of a time when you knew your truth but were afraid to speak it? Think about who you were when you kept mum. Were you who you really are? Were you of any value to the folks around you when you chose to bury your truth?

I was sitting with a therapist whom I had gone to see because I was unhappy with my life and was trying to make myself happy. I remember saying to her, "Maybe I'll go to law school or get my MBA" (two things I really didn't want), and all the while, flitting across my mind was the rather unwanted thought: "I think I'm gay." I was burying my truth and, trust me, it was making me and everyone around me miserable—except the therapist, whose income increased every time I walked out of her office still withholding the secret of what I wanted.

Bottom line, if you believe in your truth and allow it, you will be happy. When you are happy, you are creating happy experiences in your life. When you are creating happy experiences in your life, those around you are happier for it, too!

So, the belief that your truth is the only truth will ensure you are creating what you really want from the start. It also assists with the adoption of the rest of these foundational beliefs.

I Am Not My Current Circumstance; I Am Its Creator

A client of mine, Julia, was struggling. She wanted more income from her business, but it just wasn't happening. She was getting deeper and deeper into that wonderful negative thought–negative feeling cycle we've all been in.

What Julia was really doing was personalizing her

financial situation. When you personalize, you jeopardize. We are *not* terrible people because we can't pay a bill. We are *not* rotten because we didn't get a client. We are *not* going to hell because we don't have enough money to buy a cup of coffee.

We are creators having experiences we created! The more we personalize an experience, the more we stay in the feeling muck of what we don't want, thereby attracting more of it. Luckily, as creators, we can simply choose to change the experience.

So, Julia decided that she was much more than her current income and got her attention back on what she wanted: more income. She released the old idea of not having money and started creating an experience in which she had all the income she really wanted.

So Julia decided to let go of her crippling personalization of her financial circumstances and chose instead to start feeling wealthy. Since she was so wealthy now in her script, she decided to blow $5 on a scratch ticket, just for fun. Why not? After all, she had the money, and she was wealthy anyway, right? Well, she hit $500! She chose a new creation, being wealthy, and it paid off. Now she experiences income coming in from all different sources. When Julia changed her attention from *being* her circumstance to being the person *experiencing* a circumstance, she was able to generate positive thoughts and feelings that created an opportunity to attract more of what she wanted: income!

Believing that you are not your current circumstance and understanding that you can change your current creation keeps you on track even when you start to feel that things aren't going your way. If you don't like what's in front of you, don't personalize it; simply choose to create something else!

I Am Connected to My Creation
Partner through My Thoughts and Feelings

Where did the airplane come from? Orville and Wilbur weren't standing on the tarmac at Kennedy International Airport, looking up at a 747 when they thought, "Wouldn't it be great if we could fly through the air?"

Think about it: everything had to come from somewhere. No matter what you believe, it all came from somewhere, and that somewhere is the unseen. Lots of folks call it the universe, or God, or the source, or a higher power. In fact, it doesn't matter what you call it, but everything comes from it. And you are part of it. Think of it: even you came from the unseen!

How do we connect with this source and start to graciously take what we want from the unlimited storehouse that is our life? *Excuse Me* was an instruction manual for connecting with and drawing out of this unseen source, your creation partner, and all that you choose with your thoughts and feelings.

Putting attention on this belief—*I am connected to my creation partner through my thoughts and feelings*—ensures that you stay consciously connected all the time, not just for that first 16 seconds.

How would your experience change if you truly believed . . .

> All my thoughts and feelings are creative and connected to my creation partner. When I think and feel in alignment with what I am wanting, then my creation partner hears me loud and clear and begins creating the people, circumstances, events, and money that will bring what I want into my physical reality, without fail!

This is what connecting to your creation partner is all about!

My Creation Partner Wants and Provides
All I Choose for Myself without Fail

How comforting is that? And since your truth is *the* truth, why not just go for this one and believe? I know, it's easy to tell ourselves, "But what if I don't choose right?" or "I don't deserve what I am asking for" or "It's not right to ask for it."

In response to those questions, I ask you: if an "unworthy" person and a "worthy" person jumped off a hundred-story building, which one would hit the ground first? The answer is that it doesn't really matter. The Law of Gravity doesn't care if you feel worthy or not; if you jump off a building, you're going to hit the ground!

It's the same with the Law of Attraction: if you ask for and keep your attention on what you want, the universe has no choice but to provide it for you! It may not be exactly as you thought, but take a closer look, and you will find that at the highest level it is exactly what you ordered.

You can't choose "wrong" when it comes to the universe; you can only choose to receive consciously or unconsciously. If you choose to create unconsciously, you will get what you want, but it may not end up being what you thought you wanted. Don't blame your creation partner; it can only deliver what you say you want. Simply choose to create consciously, and you will easily recognize that you do indeed get what you want, even if at first it doesn't appear to be what you want.

I Have Complete Free Will, and I Know That Nothing Can Be Done *to* Me; It Has to Come *through* Me

Some folks experience trouble with creating because they think that something is going to do something to them and that what they want is just going to show up. Now, don't get me wrong, if you really believe that things will just show up, it will probably feel like they do.

However, once we understand that things happen *through* us, we can start to recognize the signs and feel the inner promptings that are guiding us toward what we want. If we think that our desires are just going to be dropped in front of us, but we don't really feel they will, we are stalling our desired results. We are pushing the gas and the brakes at the same time.

Opening your mind to the fact that your creation partner works through you will help to open your eyes to all the circumstances, people, and events it has put in place to deliver your desire to you. Always remember, your thoughts and feelings are the cause, and the effect is the experience you desire.

Ever wonder how it is possible that we can look right at people but we don't recognize them until they say something to us? Clearly, when we do this, we are not in the moment and therefore can't see what is right in front of us. This is what happened to Julia:

Julia loves white rocks, and she often looks for them on the beach. One day, she was searching and searching, but was finding every other color but white. She felt frustrated and decided to close her eyes and see only white rocks in her imagination. When she opened her eyes, she saw white rocks dotted all over the beach.

When Julia decided to calm her frustration, she was making a conscious choice to connect with her creation partner and let it work through her. When she did, she got results!

I Can Be, Do, or Have Anything

If you truly believe the first five beliefs, then this one will be true for you without question! Enough said.

Everything Is Unfolding Perfectly for Me Now
This is my favorite!

A few days ago I decided to play with the creation principles for a free cup of coffee. I got into the feeling of accepting and drinking my free cup of coffee. It tasted delicious and flavorful, and it had that magical first-cup-in-the-morning smell. I thanked the universe and put my attention on allowing it to come into my experience.

The next day I bought my morning coffee, got into my car, and the lid popped off. Needless to say, the coffee went flying all over me and the car. Now I had a choice—I could get angry and frustrated, or I could accept that this happened and simply take care of it.

I went back to the coffee shop, told them what happened, and asked if they could replace the cup of coffee while I went to the bathroom to clean up. When I came back, the clerk handed me another cup of coffee and a coupon for a free one!

If I had gotten frustrated and blamed the poor person who didn't put the lid on properly, do you think he would have taken the extra step to give me the coupon? No way! Because I didn't judge the situation as good or bad, I allowed what the universe had intended—to deliver me a free cup of coffee. The exact means weren't my choice, but it all worked out in the end!

Remember, if you believe you are connected to your creation partner, you can see how beautifully this works. When you feel good, you are always creating what you want. So, basically, you can have your coffee and drink it, too.

Congratulations! Your willingness to create these beliefs is your ticket to eliminating the things that keep you unconscious, the ugly trilogy of fear, worry, and doubt.

Let's think about it for a moment . . .

If you appreciate your truth, then you can believe all of the remaining six beliefs with ease. If you believe that you are not your current circumstances, and that you are their creator instead, you know that you create all there is with your creation partner through your thoughts and feelings. And if you believe that your creation partner wants to deliver for you all that you choose for yourself, then you would have to believe that you can be, do, and have all that you want to experience. Therefore, everything has to be unfolding perfectly!

So, I suggest that you make an agreement with your creation partner. Agree to do your part, and trust and believe it to do its part, too. Your agreement could go something like this . . .

"Today I enter into a partnership with my creation partner. I promise to always honor, speak, and act my truth so that I am clear on what I am choosing for myself. I agree to willingly create from this point forward, without judgment, exactly what I choose for myself, knowing that it will be delivered to me without fail. I will keep my thoughts and feelings centered on what I choose, knowing that I don't have to see it now, and that real work is being done in the unseen, and all will be delivered through me. Now that I know this, all circumstances and events have to be unfolding perfectly in the direction of what I have chosen. Being in this partnership, I now know that I can be, do, or have anything I choose."

When you enter into an agreement like this, how could you ever believe again that . . .

• there is never enough?

- you have no control?
- some people have all the luck?
- life is hard?

How could you?

Keep another important point in mind: accept those old limiting beliefs you have, even love them! If you choose to resist them, they will persist in your consciousness, and this is not about a duel between the old beliefs and the new ones. This is about choosing new beliefs that will ultimately replace the old ones. The last thing we want to start is a battle of beliefs in your head!

What happens when you not only believe, but start to live according to these beliefs? Magical things happen, like what happened to Lisa . . .

In Walpole, New Hampshire, I lost a gold earring the shape of a grain of wheat. It slipped out of my ear on the way to a Christmas party, somewhere during the mile walk from the office. Or maybe it slipped when I took off my scarf in the entrance hall. Everyone at the party looked around for a while, and later I traced my steps back to the office, but I couldn't find the earring. The snow was thick on the ground.

A few years before, I had read *Excuse Me, Your Life Is Waiting,* and so I focused on the joy of the moment of finding the earring.

We left the party that evening, and I worked through the rest of the winter. It snowed and it snowed. Whenever I thought of the earring, I switched glum feelings into a feeling of the confidence and gratitude I would feel at the moment of having the earring back again. Months passed, and the snow turned into slush.

One morning in early spring, someone in the office said she saw something glinting in a dirty slush pile beside the road a few blocks from the office. It was my earring!

Imagine if you were to approach your life with the same clarity about what you have chosen to experience, trusting your creation partner with the "hows"—you'd be guaranteed all that you desire!

Start today by believing the seven Creation Foundation Beliefs. Simply take each one and affirm it with powerful, positive feelings, not just once a day, but when you find yourself in circumstances that seem to contradict what you have chosen to create. Say them out loud. Use them to replace any old limiting beliefs. Say them when you're happy or fearful, when things are going well, or when you are filled with doubt.

And then allow the magic to happen!

Creation Principles Really Work!

"I had been trying to figure out how I could take a leave of absence from my career and still have enough money. I had been saving some money, but worried whether I had enough. Circumstances were becoming more stressful at work, and they were beginning to affect my health. I knew in my heart that I had to believe and have faith that the money would come, so I finally asked for the leave . . . and it was granted. Two weeks later, a check came in the mail. It was a gift from a family member for $22,000! I was so excited! I had made the decision to take care of myself and let go, knowing somehow that the money would flow, and it did!"—Carolyn

THREE

Putting You and Your Unfulfilled Intention to the Immediate Test

> You never again have to believe that it is
> wrong to want.
>
> —Lynn Grabhorn,
> *Excuse Me, Your Life Is Waiting*

With your new beliefs under your belt, it's time to take one of your unfulfilled intentions and put it (and yourself) through the creation process step by step. Your goal is to identify how you may be resisting what you have chosen to experience. Once you can identify the sources of your resistance, you can easily choose to create in the opposite direction.

Let's take a look at how Vivian, a massage therapist, started creating her reality using the creation principles . . .

Vivian had wanted to take a family vacation to Florida for a long time. Now, this wasn't just a vacation where you hop on a plane and arrive. This "vacation creation" included manifesting an RV! While Vivian knew this was a tall order, she moved past that feeling and got down to the business of creating.

First, she spent time getting perfectly clear on what her vacation would look and feel like. She pictured her family in the RV having a great time. She envisioned the places along the way where they would stop. She imagined what they would do when they got to Florida and how they would all feel once they arrived at the final destination. By the time she was done understanding what she wanted to create, she had created a script that felt so amazingly good, it was like she had already "been there, done that." She was "buzzing" big time!

Not only did she envision her script every free moment of every day, she also cut out pictures of the RV she wanted and the places she wanted to visit. She even made a "vacation banner" that she hung up in the house to encourage her family to get involved with her in the creation process.

It seemed to be the perfect conscious creation plan, but only a little progress was being made toward reaching her goal. After several months of mediocre results, Vivian took her conscious creation to the next level. While driving and wondering why things weren't coming in to support her desire, she realized that she was struggling with being a good receiver. Sure, the little things were coming in, but she had a hard time being gracious about receiving even those things.

This was her resistance! In that moment, Vivian made a clear choice to become conscious about receiving without guilt.

One day, Vivian arrived at a client's house and gave a great massage. When she was done, her client handed her a check for her work. Then her client handed her another check! Without even opening it, Vivian asked her client why there was another check. The client said that she loved hearing Vivian's excitement about her vacation so much that she wanted to help Vivian with her dream. In the past, Vivian would've felt guilty about this gift and tried to give it back, but since she had chosen to be a gracious receiver, she accepted the second check, which was for $1,500! And it didn't stop there. Vivian received a check from another client for $500, and another for $200. With the extra money she received, Vivian was able to make a down payment on the RV of her dreams. Needless to say, Vivian and her family had a great trip!

One of the first things that people do when they think they aren't getting results, or they start feeling resistance, is to give up. Vivian did something different—and I invite you to do the same—she stepped it up instead!

What do I mean by "step it up"? I mean to become conscious of where you may be experiencing resistance, and then putting your attention on creating the opposite of that resistance. When Vivian wasn't getting the results she wanted, she didn't give up on her vacation; she just stepped up her understanding of how she might have been resisting the process of creation. She didn't blame her creation partner; rather, she looked at what *she* could change. By being conscious and identifying her resistance to receiving, she was able to clear the resistance and allow her desire to come into her experience.

How many times have you chosen to give up when you weren't getting the results you wanted? Trust me, I do it all the time. Now imagine if, instead of blaming your creation partner, you looked at what might be preventing you from allowing what you desire into your experience. Do you think that things might change? Try it and see! When things don't seem to be going your way, put your attention on "stepping it up," not "giving up" on your creation!

Another thing that people do when they feel resistance is to settle for less than what they wanted. Vivian actually had more than enough money to fly her whole family to Florida, but that wasn't what she really wanted to create. She could have easily changed her desire, but she believed in herself and these principles, and she ultimately got exactly what she wanted! Now, let's look at what happens when you downgrade your intention:

Lori set an intention to have a new eight-seat vehicle. All along, she was excited about the fact that it was new and spacious. After she put her attention on having this vehicle for a while, her aunt contacted her and said that she was selling her minivan—which just happened to be the model that Lori wanted. But her aunt's vehicle was used, and Lori wanted a new one. Instead of thanking her aunt for the offer and turning her down because it didn't align with her intention, Lori did what we all tend to do—she started to question her original intention. When Lori talked about having the new car, you could hear the excitement in her voice. When she talked about maybe buying the used car, you could hear the disappointment in her voice. How Lori was feeling was a clear indication of the direction she ought to go in next, but like many of us, she tried to talk herself into settling for less.

I am not saying that it is never okay to change your original intention. If downgrading your intention still makes you feel good—perhaps you're offered a different option you hadn't considered before—then by all means, go for it! But if you're feeling less-than-good about downgrading, it's not the way to go.

Someone once said, "If we could just keep our attention on having what we want until we get it, we would have everything that we wanted." It's a simple and true statement. So when you feel resistance, don't give up—step it up! Don't downgrade—upgrade! This is the way to consciously move past your resistance and keep your positive energy flowing in the direction you have chosen.

Now let's look at some other ways you might be losing your focus and sabotaging your intention.

Do You Know What You *Really* Want?

So what is your unfulfilled intention? For example, do you want . . .

- to lose that last ten pounds?
- a million dollars?
- to make a living doing work you love?
- to have your ideal relationship?
- a red Ferrari?
- your business to take off?

What is it? Is it written down? If not, write it down now and let's get started!

Now answer the following question completely honestly, and remember your truth is your truth:

Is this what I *really* want?

When I was just out of college, a career counselor asked me what I wanted, and I said that I wanted to earn a million dollars by the time I was 30. Did I really want a million dollars? No, but at the time it sounded good. I also said that I wanted to be a high-powered businessperson. Again, not true. These were things I was being told I should want, and because I didn't trust my own truth, I set my intentions on these un-truths. What I really wanted was to earn a living by helping people. Did I make the million? Nope! Did I become a high-powered businessperson? Nope. Do I make a living helping people? Yep, but only after 15 years of toiling in corporate America because my original intention was not what I really wanted.

This is a form of self-sabotage: you say you want something, but you don't do the things you need to do to have it. I said I wanted a million dollars, but because it really wasn't what I wanted, I didn't do the things I should have done to make it happen. I was actually doing a form of self-preservation. I was unconsciously choosing to not create what I really didn't want.

Many folks have come to me and said that they don't understand why their intention is not coming into their experience. Together, we have uncovered that their intention is not what they really wanted to start with.

So, is your unfulfilled intention something you *really* want, or is it a "should," a "have-to," or, even worse, a "need-to" in disguise? Bottom line, you don't feel good when you are focused on a "should," "have-to," or "need-to," and therefore you are sending out mixed signals and will not create what you've intended.

If this is the case with your intention, then take another stab at identifying the experience you really, truly want to create. Here's an example:

Christina owns a cosmetics company. One of her marketing ideas was to sell her products on an at-home shopping network. Her intention was to meet and exceed her sales goals. Her products were selling well, but she still wasn't reaching the goals established by the network. Needless to say, she was frustrated!

I asked Christina a simple question, "What do you really want to get out of this home shopping network experience?" Without hesitation, she said that she really loved being in front of the camera and connecting with the in-house audience. She wanted to experience more of that. So she changed her intention from her "should"—to meet and exceed her sales goals—to really enjoying every moment of her on-camera experience.

The next day, she still had her sales goal of three thousand units, but she chose to go forward with her new intention to basically enjoy herself and the audience. She was on for only seven minutes, and she sold six thousand units!

Once Christina was able to focus her attention on what she really wanted, the sales took care of themselves. Why? Because once you choose what you *really* want to experience, you feel great, which sends out clear signals to your creation partner that this is really what you want. Christina wanted to experience a connection with the audience. When she did, her creation partner made sure she would have another opportunity to do it again by ensuring that she met her sales goals.

So, again, is your intention what you *really* want, or what you think you should want? Your truth is your truth, so you will increase your chances of consistently successful creation if you start there!

Does Your Intention Make You *Feel* Good?

Now, does the way you stated your intention feel good to you? If it doesn't, you're going to resist it coming to you. I spoke with someone the other day who said she wanted to lose ten pounds. I asked her how that felt and, of course, she said it felt terrible. I thought of her dragging herself to the gym at 5:00 A.M. to hop on a treadmill. Just the thought of it made her so depressed that she wanted to eat a whole box of Ring-Dings. Talk about resistance!

As I mentioned before, Lynn referred to these types of intentions as "negative wants"—they seem to be what you want, but when you state them as your intention, they don't feel so good.

"I intend to lose ten pounds." *Bad.*

"I intend to find a way to be healthier that I enjoy." *Good!*

"I intend to start a job search." Yuck (the thought of that makes my stomach turn).

"I intend to create work I love." *Good!*

"I intend to start dating." *Bad.*

"I intend to create my ideal relationship." *Good!*

How does your unfulfilled intention make you feel? Is there room to "buzz it up" with even more feeling? Rewrite it and be sure the mere thought of it makes you smile. Turn a negative into a positive. Your intention has got to really get you jazzed or else you won't be excited to tackle the next step—reviewing your script.

How Does Your Script Stand Up?

You have now ensured that your unfulfilled intention is what you really want and you have written it in a way that gives you great positive energy. Knowing and being clear about what you really want gets you really conscious, and when you are really conscious you know that you are right on track! Now it's time to write your script about your intention.

Lynn describes scripting as "concocting a present-time whimsical narration about your want, spoken out loud (writing is the second choice) as if chatting with a friend. It must never, never be about what is *going* to happen . . . only about what *has* or *is* happening now. And you make the telling of this real enough you can taste the satisfaction, enjoyment, fulfillment and joy in every nuance, every increment as you muse along."

So, how does the script for your unfulfilled intention stand up? First, let's look at Carolyn's story:

Carolyn N. is a published author now ready to publish what she considers to be her most valuable work—her gift to the world. Carolyn doesn't enjoy working with publishers—in fact, she downright hates it.

When I first spoke with her, it was all about what she didn't want in a publishing relationship. She was actually considering self-publishing because, as she put it, "the material is quite a bit out of the mainstream of books being published. This is my seventh book, and all the others have been published the normal way. This one is more radical than the others, I think, so even if it does find a publisher out there, I want to help it along in the world."

She didn't want the publisher to have all the control over the writing, cover art, and layout. She didn't want to have to deal with them during the publishing process. She didn't want a publisher at all, but she felt that the message of her book was so important that it needed to get to the largest possible audience, and therefore it would need the added strength of a publisher.

After some cajoling, Carolyn was willing to take a stab at scripting her ideal publishing relationship. Here is what she started with:

My new book, *Ecstatic Relations,* is enthusiastically sought after by more than one publisher, which makes it possible for me to call the artistic shots. I design and produce the book with my own collaborators, and the publisher markets and distributes it widely. It stays in print for the next ten years; I have an unlimited number of copies to give away; I am paid well; it becomes a cult book that people share with each other; libraries all over the country stock it. It leads to people wishing to work with me. They use my work in their own work, and some of them become true friends of the heart. I am introduced to communities all over the country, meet the housewives who harbor their hopes in secret, the truck drivers with dreams of their own, the teenagers who long for somebody who understands what they're talking about. Books I have produced over the past 30 years are sought after, some are reprinted, and all are widely distributed and read.

Shortly after writing her script, Carolyn got a letter from a publisher she had sent her manuscript to three months before. In the letter, the publisher offered her the opportunity to co-publish the book; both the publisher and author would take partial responsibility for the production and release of the book. This was the start of what Carolyn had scripted!

Carolyn sent a letter back to the publisher stating her additional requirements:

"Thank you for your offer. In fact, collaborating with a publisher would be the best of all possible options for me. I wonder, though, if you wouldn't consider a somewhat alternative arrangement like the following: I prepare the book for printing—with a professional book designer, cover artist, copy editor, whom I will pay directly—and send the publisher a camera-ready manuscript when that's done in mid-November, I would guess. (In fact, the job is already underway, with very talented people I've worked with before. We want the book to be a work of art in itself.) Of course, I would consult with you on every decision, and you could accept some and reject others—in other words, we'd collaborate. Since this book is my response to the world situation, it's very important to me that it get out there in a timely manner and be read by many, many people. I want the medium to be the message (a work of creative collaboration, beautiful to look at, fun, educational . . .). I happen to love the process of creating a book with friends, so I want this to be an inspiring experience for everyone working on it.

Remember, Carolyn was not one to believe that she could ever have an ideal publishing relationship, but because she was willing to script the possibility of it, she was well on her way to creating it! More on Carolyn's story in a little bit . . .

Scripting is the opportunity to open up to possibilities that we would never have believed possible due to our limited prior experiences. Carolyn was dead-set against the idea of an ideal publishing relationship. Once she opened up and really understood what she wanted, she could then simply put her attention on it with powerful feelings and allow it to come into her experience.

So what about your script? Have you written one? Do you say it out loud? Does it make you feel so good that you "buzz" with excitement every time you think of it?

Be sure, as with your intention, that everything you have written in your script is what you really want. Carolyn could easily have written a script based on what she "thought" she could have versus what she really wanted, but her creation would have been along the lines of what she didn't want. Does your script include your "ideal" results?

Now that you see the importance of ensuring that your script is focused on what you want, not on what you think you can have, go through your description and take out anything that feels like a "don't want," a "should," or a "have-to." Add in all of the things you want, but that maybe you thought were asking too much. Then see how it feels when you read it out loud!

Remember these three requirements when writing or rewriting your script:

1. It has to feel GREAT.
2. It has to be believable to you.
3. It has to be in the present, positive tense ("I am" versus "I will").

The way to ensure that you will meet these three requirements is not to put any attention whatsoever on how this is going to be your experience. As soon as you start thinking about the "hows," doubts begin to creep into your mind, and you limit yourself.

Please, please, please remember, it is the job of your creation partner to deliver the people, circumstances, and events that will bring about the experience you are scripting. Your job is merely to get clear, stay clear, and get out of the way!

Are You Too Focused on the "How"?

Let's say you write a simple script about having a new TV: "I am so happy and grateful now that I am sitting here watching my new 65-inch projection TV. I love sitting with my remote, channel surfing, and eating my popcorn." Then let's say you start wondering about where you are going to find the money to pay for this beauty! When we are thinking about creating something, we often go straight to the question of where the money is going to come from—the "how." But money is a very limiting "how"! By putting your attention on money, you are, in essence, binding the hands of your creation partner. What if someone gave you the TV as a present? What if you won it in a raffle? What if you found it on the side of the road intact and ready to go? We don't know how our creation partner is going to deliver it—so why would we want to limit how it will come?

Also, keep in mind that when you are focused on the

"how," you do not have your attention on already having it. So, by the Law of Attraction, you will get more worries about how, not having. Furthermore, when you are focused on the fact that you don't have the money, you don't feel good. And when you feel badly, you are letting your creative power just ooze away from you.

So now that your attention is off the "how," is your script believable? You'll know by feeling, not thinking; your script has to feel believable to you. You may wonder how specific to get when you're scripting. The answer is to get as specific as you can believe. Again, it all comes down to feelings. If you feel your script is believable, it is. If you feel your script is not believable, it isn't, and therefore you will create resistance.

There's a great song by musical artist Alanis Morrisette called "21 Things I Want in a Lover." In it, she basically laundry-lists all of the qualities of the person she would like to be with next. She's pretty specific, but it's still believable because she says that they're "not necessarily needs, but qualities that I prefer." Now, I don't know Alanis, but I'd venture to guess that the previous statement made the list believable to her.

If you'd like to stay a little more general than Alanis, you could script something more bare-bones like, "I am so happy and grateful now that I am in a partnership filled with love, companionship, and fulfillment." This is not very specific, but it certainly captures the essence of what you choose to create next.

There is a story about a woman who went to her prayer group and asked them to pray that a specific man would marry her. Several months later, she came back to thank them because she had married the man. A couple of months after that, the story goes, she went back and asked her prayer group to pray to get rid of him! Needless to say, perhaps this woman's intention was originally too specific.

So how specific should you be? It's up to you, but remember your new belief that the universe provides what you choose without fail. Since that is your truth, the only person you have to convince through scripting is yourself!

How Detailed Is Your Script?

Another question people ask about scripting is, "Do I script the end result, or just what I want step by step?" By now you know what I am going to ask next: "What do you feel will work best for you?" Some folks do a step-by-step process, while others only put their attention on seeing the end result.

Carolyn, the author I introduced you to earlier in this chapter, implemented the step-by-step strategy. During the proposal process with her publisher, she created a new script for the next stage of the creation of her book.

My potential publisher, in a timely manner, accepts my proposal to design and prepare *Ecstatic Relations* for printing, using my own designer and artists. They offer proofreading and have an excellent reader who does the job skillfully and rapidly. The book is ready to go into printing by December first.

They send the manuscript to several well-known people for blurbs, and the response is enthusiastic. A momentum of enthusiasm and anticipation builds even before the book is out. My work with Sara (the editor) is healing for both of us; collaborating with Sharon (the artist) is as important to her as it is to me. The piece she makes for the cover is so touching, it makes me cry. The energy of our collaboration is effectively contagious, and it raises the mood and energy of all the people around us.

I am open to the editing ideas and suggestions of my readers, but I remain true to my own vision for this book. I never forget why I'm doing it or what my prayer for it is in the world. The medium is the message at every stage, and it effectively touches the lives of the people who come into its path.

Skillful means are utilized at every stage. Pleasure, creativity, and fun are present for everyone working on it. It is a joy-bringer. Synchronicities abound, and as if by magic the right people and the right opportunities appear at all the right moments. Surprises also abound, and the whole experience is an adventure for everyone working on it—which is a lot of people. All of them wish to share the excitement, and so the word gets around and its effect is, in general, encouragement, self-acceptance, reassurance, and spreading warmth. Hearts are opened, bit by bit, including my own.

I am humbled by the power of this process, but not immodest. My ambition is that the book be nothing less than a world-changer, person by person, as hearts and minds respond to the stories, as consciousness wakes up a little bit more, as light filters in and the community of fellow workers in this realm find me through the book, and therefore find each other. And we join hands, making the web that much stronger . . .

The design prototype is on its way. I'm intending that the publisher will be relieved that she doesn't have to do the work, will decide that it is beautiful, and will give us a carte blanche to continue preparing the book. Also, she will make an exception and agree to read the manuscript soon, so that it can come out in spring rather than next fall. She will sign a contract and give me everything I've asked for, none of which is unreasonable or selfish. When I've heard back from them (a miracle in itself!), I'll set up another meeting to prepare for the next steps.

I received an e-mail last December from Carolyn:

The book is going into production in January, and the publisher is amazingly flexible in response to all my requests. I even suggested we try and print the book on non-wood pulp paper, and if it's not too expensive, she's up for it. I told her I wished the medium to be the message at every stage, and she agreed to it. I get to design the book and to have a say in who and how it gets printed. They'll do all the grunt work of copy-editing, publicity, and distribution. It looks like it's working!

It's getting harder to tell whether we are reading Carolyn's scripts or if we are reading what is happening in her "reality."

I heard from Carolyn again in April of this year:

My new book is deep in production right now, and it's going along almost as well as I could have wished. Now, I'm planning to bring all my out-of-print books back as e-books, and they should come out around the same time as the new one.

Things seem to be working out in most every way I had envisioned. Not only the new book, but also three of my previously printed books are coming out again as e-books (that was a whole other script) with no cost to me! And all four books will come onto the scene at about the same time. Magic is definitely in the air!

Now Carolyn is off to script her ideal marketing plan for her books. Do you think she will create what she scripts? You bet she will! In fact, Carolyn's book, *Ecstatic Relations,* is now in bookstores!

If it feels good to script in stages, go for it. If it feels better to simply envision the end result, then do that. Your test is always whether or not it feels good and is believable to you.

So take a look at your script. Does it bring you joy and excitement when you read it? If so, then it can't help but be believable. If not, simply take out what doesn't feel good. This is your script, so you are free to add or detract as much as you choose.

Review your script by asking the following questions:

- Is my script in alignment with my intention?
- Does it make me feel good?
- Is it believable?
- Is it written in the present, positive tense?

If you answered "no" to any of these questions, go back to see where you might have been adding resistance and rewrite it!

Are You Subconsciously Focused on "Don't Wants"?

After reviewing your intention and your script, it is critical to ask one more important question: "What would be the downside of having my want?"

WHAT?

I know, I know, but bear with me . . .

We have already identified where you might be stalling your creation. You've cleared your intention and made sure that it is yours and is what you want. You have reviewed your script and molded it into great shape. Both of these steps have ensured that you can feel great about what you're creating, and help you to stay clear as the creation process unfolds.

So how come it's still not here? You are doing the first part of your job—being clear on a conscious level—but what about the subconscious level? Identifying whether you are resisting what you want at a subconscious level and scripting that may be the crux of your creation frustration.

Let's say you want a million dollars. Terrific! Now, what will you get when you have the million dollars that you don't have today? You may say things like . . .

- freedom
- certainty
- fun
- choices
- options
- relief
- no debt
- happiness
- excitement
- security

But what would be the downside of having a million dollars?

At first glance you may think, like most, that there couldn't be a downside. But dig a bit deeper and you may find yourself saying things like:

- I don't have the skills to handle that kind of money.
- I would have to work really hard to have that kind of money.
- I don't know anything about investing.
- I will lose it all.
- People will want to take it from me.
- I will lose my friends.
- I will have to pay a lot of taxes.

Hmmm, so your intention and therefore your script have a lot of hidden "don't wants" attached to them. You are sending out mixed signals that confuse your creation partner. You are resisting the very thing you say you want to create, and therefore it is not here and won't be here until your unconscious "don't wants" are cleared up.

When you look at what you want and you really can't see a downside, simply ask yourself, "What am I willing to admit might be a downside?" If there truly isn't one, then your resistance may be in the allowing step of creation, as we'll see in a little bit.

But now, let's get back to the downside. Follow the same process you used before: take your list and start turning your "don't wants" into "do wants."

"I don't have the skills to handle that kind of money" becomes "I will learn how to handle that kind of money."

"I would have to work really hard to have that kind of money" becomes "I will look for ways to have that kind of money easily."

"I don't know anything about investing" becomes "I will find someone I trust who knows about investing."

And on and on . . .

Now update your script with these new wants! Let's see how Denise did this:

D enise wants to build her dream house on the property of her existing house. This has been a dream of both her and her husband, and Denise has recently been applying the principles of creation to this intention. Denise has a script that brings her joy every time she reads it. She keeps her attention on her script and feels the excitement of living in her new house.

When I first asked Denise what her downside would be, she was quite sure that she didn't have one. But after she thought about it for a moment, she identified that when their new house was built, they would have to rent out their old one. Denise didn't realize it before, but she really doesn't like the idea of getting involved with renters. She has only heard horror stories, and on top of that, she really has no idea what is involved.

Denise became conscious of her downside! Now she could replace the fear with a description of her ideal rental situation and ensure that her original script was truly believable!

William was having similar trouble . . .

William was learning a new business that entailed multimillion-dollar transactions. William seemed to be unfazed by the staggering amounts of money involved in these deals and simply kept his intention clear—"to transact one of these deals from start to finish."

He started connecting with the right people who could help him make this transaction part of his reality. Everything would be going along smoothly, but right at the last minute, the deal would fall through for no foreseeable reason. William was stymied! He had set his intention, written a great script, things seemed to be happening, and then, all of a sudden, the deal would fail.

William asked himself what the downside would be. Of course, at first he couldn't see one—why in the world would he create a failure of a deal that would put a million dollars in his pocket? When he looked deeper, though, he realized that while he was comfortable creating all the circumstances for the deal to take place, he was uncomfortable with the circumstances that would transpire after the deal took place. He was uncomfortable with the tax and Patriot Act implications (important government regulations), which he had minimal understanding of at the present time.

William was creating what he wanted—the circumstances to make a deal like this come to fruition—but
he became conscious of the fact that he was as close to
a completed transaction as his creation partner could
take him because he feared what would happen when
the deal went through.

It was clear to William that he had to do some
rescripting. After he did, he randomly started meeting
people who could help him learn and move beyond his
resistance regarding the taxes and Patriot Act.

William is still working on his deal, and is now
completely comfortable with his intention and his
script!

So what could be your hidden "don't wants"? Could
it be that once you have what you want, you feel that
you:

- might not be able to handle the results?
- have a fear of change?
- may not deserve the results you want?
- will lose an important relationship?
- won't have time for the other important things in
  your life?

You are a creator, so now's the time to rewrite your
script, turning these into powerful "do wants." In your
new script, see yourself:

- handling the results effortlessly.
- welcoming change.
- enjoying the results because you know you deserve
  them.
- enjoying your relationships even more.
- spending time doing what you love.

You have the power to create anything you want. Now that you've identified and dealt with the sources of your resistance, the sky's the limit!

Creation Principles Really Work!

"I had to make one of the biggest decisions of my life—whether or not I should leave college my first week there. I was suffering from anxiety attacks that put me in the hospital twice. This decision would change my life forever, and the process was breaking me down both physically and mentally.

"I had seen doctors and therapists, and been prescribed medication. None of it worked. It felt as though I was going through a car wash with just water—what I needed was soap!

"One day, my father picked up *Excuse Me, Your Life Is Waiting* and suggested I read it. The day I picked up that book was the day my life made a complete change. It was as if I were turning in my old car for a brand-new one. I had my resolution! It was positive feelings, not doctors or medication—it was FEELINGS!

"The creation principles have led me to enjoying my life. I am in the driver's seat. I control my life 1,000,000,000 percent. I created a successful Web site called www.PositiveFeelingsRule.com, which focuses on teaching college students the creation principles so that they can create the life experience they really want. People from around the world are contacting me to tell me how they are changing their lives, too! It's time to spread the energy!"—Sebastian Oddo

FOUR

Becoming a Master Allower ... NOW

> You never again have to believe that some
> great power outside of yourself is pulling the
> strings, or that anyone or anything other
> than you is in control.
>
> —Lynn Grabhorn,
> *Excuse Me, Your Life Is Waiting*

Congratulations! Your unfulfilled intention has now passed the first phase of the creation process. It is powerful, positive, and fueled by a script that brings you wonderfully positive feelings, with no hidden resistance. You are doing your job well!

Your intention and your script are important tools, but what is the most important tool you have in becoming a conscious creator? YOU! Having a great intention and script does you no good if you aren't the person who is conscious of how to allow your intention to come into your experience.

This is the area where resistance rears up its head and can really turn your joy of creation into frustration. It is also the one area over which you have complete control because it is all about you—you choosing to be conscious of what you are thinking, saying, and doing!

Let's go back to our new Creation Foundation Beliefs for a moment. If your new beliefs are that "there is only one source of all there is, and I am connected to that source by my thoughts and feelings" and "I know that I have complete free will and that nothing can be done to me; it has to come through me," then you can understand how important your role as an allower is. When you are cut off from your source because you are frustrated, angry, sad, or judgmental—all those mealy feelings that come from a sense of fear—you are slowing down your creation. When you feel happy, loving, joyful, and accepting, you are connected, and life simply flows through you.

Just today, I was feeling a little fear. I shifted my attention by stating and feeling that I loved and accepted myself and all of my current circumstances, that everything was unfolding perfectly. I decided to take a break and simply started flowing positive thoughts about myself and what I was working on. As I drove to get a cup of coffee, I focused on being grateful for the moment I was experiencing, and I felt so much better than when I was flowing fear. By the time I got to the coffee shop, I felt connected again. I was in the moment. I was the only one in line. As I waited, I looked down, and a twenty-dollar bill was on the ground! Best of all, there was no one around to ask if it was theirs!

By shifting from fear to love, I was able to be in the moment and take note of what I would never have noticed if I were stewing about what I wasn't enjoying about my circumstances. Being connected means *allowing!*

Lynn talks about getting jazzed about your intention for at least 16 seconds, which is a fantastic start. And, as you really put your attention on it, you'll want to do it more because it feels so great! Remember, you are always creating, so the more you stay consciously connected to your source, the more you ensure that you are creating in a direction that you really want.

Lynn goes on to explain the difference between taking inspired action versus whacking away at a problem:

1. "Well, first comes the inspiration, the ideas. They come because you've been spending more time in those higher frequencies feeling good (or better), buzzing and turning on."

2. "Then, after flowing goodly amounts of Feel Good energy to one or more of those great new ideas, you start to act on them, yes, but now from a place of hallowed inspiration rather than negative pushing. And so your actions now become as inspired as your idea, and everything that is coming to you is coming from a place of higher frequency."

3. "Then Yeow-ee! Something amazing begins to happen. No matter how complex or involved the ideas seem to be, you find them falling into place, and flowing along with the ease and sureness of an uninterrupted mountain stream. And why not? Your ideas were inspired; now, too, are your actions to bring those ideas into reality. All from your higher-frequency energy flow."

You know the feeling of inspired action—it kind of feels like a crystal-clear stream washing through you or a flash of insight. It moves you along naturally. There isn't a whole lot of thinking involved, just natural action. The action comes directly from a source of love for yourself and your creation. Whacking comes from fear, a sense that your creation is somehow not coming.

After Bob (at the publishing house) and I decided that I should come down to Virginia to meet, I remember hanging up the phone and thinking, "How am I going to do that?" I didn't have enough money to fly and stay in a hotel. I remember recognizing that my attention was squarely on all the reasons why I *couldn't* go, instead of on the fact that I wanted to go. Once I became conscious of where my attention was, I shifted it to already having taken the trip, and then a feeling of inspiration came over me. Instead of ignoring it, which was my typical response before, I chose to allow it to come through. It's hard to describe, but it felt as though I released all the negative thoughts, which allowed a sense of calm. And out of this amazing sense of calm came a simple idea . . . Why don't you just drive, Doreen?

Twelve hours really isn't that long, I thought, so why not? Then it was as natural as putting one foot in front of the other. I was able to rearrange my work schedule, my partner could take off work to take care of our daughter, the time that would work best for me also worked for my publisher, and, on top of it all, they were kind enough to pick up the hotel tab.

From that one moment of calm flowed all the circumstances that I wanted so I could take my trip!

If I hadn't made a conscious choice to shift my attention to what I really wanted—which was to go on the trip—I would not have allowed such a simple idea to come into my head.

You know those times where you are so focused on finding a solution to something and you simply can't come up with one? And then you tell a friend, who comes up with the perfect solution? Now think about those times when you heard your friend's suggestion, but you didn't really listen. Later, after trying a hundred other solutions without much success, you found out that your friend had had the perfect solution after all.

Think of your creation partner as the friend with the good answers. Get clear and keep your attention on staying clear, so that you are able to recognize the ways in which your creation partner is flowing your desires through you. This is what allowing is all about.

So, how can we experience this flow more and more often? We can start by eliminating the "Why isn't it here yet?" syndrome by understanding that we already have what it is we *really* want.

From Need to Choice

Wouldn't it be great if you truly believed you had everything inside you that you could ever need—the means to absolute security, health, wisdom, love, peace, and abundance? How would your life change if you were always truly being who you really are and always had your attention on creating what you really want? If you were doing this, you would only attract people who complemented your life, so you wouldn't have any conflict in your relationships. If you were connected to your true abundance, you would be happy with what you had and perfectly comfortable with wanting more. If you were consciously creating what you *really* want, you would never create by default and invite "accidents" into your experience. *Life could be effortless and lived purely by choice!*

What do you think you attract when you say you need something? More need. What do you think you attract when you say you *want* something? More want.

What do you think you attract when you say that you *choose* something? The thing you have chosen.

How do you go from need to choice? Lynn narrated the exercise of helping one of her seminar participants identify why she wanted what she wanted:

In one of my weekend seminar groups, a gal spoke up with, "All right, I understand now that I've been focusing on the lack of my dream, but I can only come up with one Why."

"Okay, what is your want?"

"I want a summer cottage by the ocean." (No oomph.)

"Why?"

"Because I hate being housebound in the summer."

Ah ha, a major Don't Want. I kept asking why.

"Why don't you want to be housebound in the summer?"

"Because I like the feeling of leisure and relaxation I get from a summer house. And freedom, yes, I like the freedom."

"Good! You're starting to connect; let's keep going. Why do you like the freedom?"

"It makes me feel good . . . and happy. Oh, yes! I remember feeling so happy as a youngster in our summer home. It was a wonderful feeling."

"Now we're getting there. Tell me more; what's your summer home like?"

"Well, it's a gray Cape Cod cottage, kind of weather-beaten, but so homey. And it has white trim. Oh, how I love the crispness of that white trim."

"More. Is it close to the water?"

"Oh, yes, right on the dunes."

"Why do you want to be so close to the water?"

"Oh, because it's so soothing, even in the stormy weather. It makes me feel real and alive. I can paint there, and watch the sunsets, and lose myself in the vastness of it all, and, well, everything just comes alive in me by the sea."

Yes! Finally this gal was cooking on the front burner! Her juices were running, and her vibrational frequencies were becoming higher and higher, magnetically charging up that growing Want-thought with every new thought she fed it.

Lynn's purpose for getting this young woman to identify her "whys" was to help her to build a powerful, positive script. And there's more, too. Let's take a closer look at what this exercise is really about by answering one simple question: *Do you think this young woman would want her beach house if, when she got it, she DIDN'T feel freedom, happiness, realness, and aliveness?*

Now, I ask you, if you didn't get the good feelings you thought you would have when you actually got what you say you want, would you still want it? Probably not.

In the end, you never really want the thing you say you want. You want the feelings you think it will bring you. Yes, this woman wanted the house, but what she thought she would ultimately get from the house were the feelings of freedom, happiness, realness, and aliveness. To feel these feelings—that's what she really wanted, and that's what you really want, too!

What does this have to do with needing and choosing?

Notice one very important thing—she was already able to feel those feelings without having the house. While she was speaking, she was actually experiencing the feelings of freedom, happiness, realness, and aliveness in that moment, without actually having the house. She already had what she ultimately wanted. THIS IS YOUR POWER, TOO!

Since you already have what you want when you

read your script and "buzz"—the feelings—you don't *need* the actual experience. You may still *want* the experience, but now you are in a position of power because you can simply *choose* to experience it.

The new car, boat, career, and relationship are all experiences; they are not the reason you feel anything. Feelings have to come from within you. How many times have you wanted something, got it, and then felt the same, as if you never had it? The reason is because your feelings are who you are, not what you have!

Getting a book contract should have been one of the most exciting times of my life, but I was still feeling badly about myself because I was still in financial trouble and my relationship was suffering. Then the money started to come in, but I was still feeling badly because the relationship was still suffering. I was choosing to attract certain experiences—the book deal and more money—but I was still not feeling great even though I was attracting those things. They couldn't make me feel happiness. The experience of having what you want can enhance your happiness, but it has no power to create it—only you do.

If you have what you really want—the good feelings—the pressure is off. You can simply choose to experience more of the experiences that you think will bring you more happiness. Now your wants are choices. How cool is that?

So, according to the Law of Attraction, if the young woman who wants a beach house continues to feel free, happy, real, and alive NOW, she will attract those things that she believes will support those feelings, like a BEACH HOUSE! That's how it works. You have always had the power to attract all you want because you already actually have what you ultimately want inside you right now.

I know, you may be saying to yourself, this is all well and good and even exciting, but how come I still think

I need the house? Because you have always been taught to seek what you want outside of yourself. You were never encouraged to see the truth: you really do have all that you need to create any experience that you could ever want inside you right now—there is no lapse in time! This is the road to experiencing everything that comes into your life as magical!

Jeff went from homeless teen to published author by *being* before *having*:

I remember those days clearly, cramped in the front seat of our two-door Buick. My mother and I shared the space with our pet cockatiel, my turtle, our goldfish in a cup, and our four bedrooms' worth of stuff crammed in the back seat. I never for once ever imagined people like us would end up homeless. That was for "them," for "those people," but it was happening, and I was living every painful moment of it.

Washing my dirty socks in the muddy water that drained into the street gutters, and getting up early and going to the grocery store praying there would be samples for us to eat—I remember it all too well, and it was quite frankly the lowest point of my life. It was hard for me, and hard for my mother, but I think it was even harder for my little brother. Kids would whisper just loud enough for us to hear, "Are they sleeping in their car?" They would say that as they peered inside to take a better look, talking about us like we were dirt.

I was so embarrassed. I wrote my thoughts in a journal. I kept writing and believing that one day, somehow, we would get out of that horrible situation, and my dreams would come true. I would be a successful author, but how and when? Didn't God hear our prayers?

Somebody heard our prayers because we did make it out of that situation, step by step. I kept writing, but I kept struggling until one of my dearest friends, producer Kathy Wilson, gifted me with a copy of *Excuse*

Me, Your Life Is Waiting by Lynn Grabhorn for my 26th birthday. I didn't know what to make of the book, but I thought I'd give it a quick read. I thought it would be just another one of those self-help, positive-thinking books, but it was so much more. It was a book that changed my life, literally, and a book that I recommend to everyone I know.

For years, I struggled to get my story, "Forever My Lady," off the ground. It tells the story of a juvenile delinquent who struggles to turn his life around. I tried to get it to become a film, but after rejection and more rejection, and after reading the *Excuse Me* book, I decided to make it a novel. I decided to FEEL the readers loving the book page by page, FEEL them connecting with the characters. I decided to self-publish the book just like Lynn Grabhorn did initially with her *Excuse Me* book, and then I would FEEL a big publishing company picking up the novel and taking it to the next level. How in the world that would happen I had no idea, but I knew what I wanted, and what I didn't want. I kept "buzzing" and feeling jazzed about everything that was happening, no matter how small it might have been. I FELT my way into the hands of the perfect agent and got her!

But the thing I wanted most of all was to FEEL my way into having the perfect publishing company pick it up. I knew everything was against me—statistics show that you have to do things a certain way and big publishing companies just don't pick up self-published books—but I kept FEELING it. One night, I decided to FEEL a particular editor (who we'd sent the book off to) reading the book and loving it. The editor's name was Andie, and she worked for a company called Warner Books. The next morning, I received a call at my job from my agent telling me that Andie wanted to pick up "Forever My Lady" for Warner Books.

I was "buzzing." It felt so surreal because it was just as I had visualized, just as I had FELT it happening. It really does work. I had to pinch myself because even this kid who lived in his car, who begged for samples to eat at grocery stores, even this kid with nothing but a hope that somehow things would get better could FEEL his way into success. Even this kid could have his dreams come true.

Jeff already had what he wanted—the feeling of having his book picked up by a major publisher. With his attention on *being* those feelings, he allowed his creation partner to set the stage for what Jeff had identified as an experience that would generate more of the feelings he was already having.

Okay, now what do *you* do? You put your attention on *being* the feelings today that you think you will have when you have what you want. Go back to your script and pull out the feelings you identified that you will feel when your want comes into your experience. Will you feel:

- happy?
- successful?
- free?
- important?
- secure?
- joyful?
- proud?
- excited?

Write up your list of feelings and start putting your attention on being those feelings today. Again, this is not about experiencing something and then feeling happy; it's about being happy and then experiencing more happiness.

Start with your script. Read it as though you are choosing it, not wanting it. Then spend your day intentionally feeling happy, or free, or excited, or grateful, or whatever feeling you are able to be without a lot of work.

Let's say the feelings you identified are:

• natural
• effortless
• fun/happy
• balanced
• grateful

From these feelings, create a being script: "I am so happy and grateful now that I am being balanced in all that I do. That I am happy and having fun in all that I do. I love that I am being effortless."

The art of allowing is being the person who already has what you choose to experience before it actually comes into physical reality. In doing this, you are now well on the way to becoming a master of the Law of Attraction!

According to Lynn, "The key to having whatever your most divine heart desires—bar nothing—is finding a way to feel good about your want: not wish for it, yearn for it, long for it, sigh for it, or feel discouraged about it, but just feel good about it."

The way to feel good all the time—to actually become the person who already has your want—is by getting conscious about your thoughts, words, and actions. The more your thoughts, words, and actions are in alignment with what you have chosen, the faster you will attract it into your experience.

You have a choice, a very important choice: you can choose to believe that something is a part of your life only when you actually see it before you with your two eyes, or you can choose to believe that something is in your reality when you see and feel it in your mind's eye. Of course, if you are waiting for it to show up, you are attracting more "showing up." If you see and feel it in your mind's eye and simply know that it has to come into your physical reality, then, in actuality, it is already here!

I know, this is a big shift in perspective, but please bear with me. It will be worth it, I promise.

Because your script is based on having what you want, you have already started putting your attention on sustaining the feelings that your script conjures up for you. Now it's time to not only feel those feelings, but to consciously think, speak, and act them as well.

Thoughts

If your current belief is that . . .

- life happens;
- I have no control;
- there is a greater power that runs my life;
- I have a purpose that I have to figure out;
- we ultimately have no choice;
- I have some control, but certainly not all of the control,

. . . then you are not a person who already has what you want—and you never will be if you continue to think this way. To be a person who already has what you want you must believe and think about the Creation Foundation Beliefs:

- The only truth is my truth.
- I am not my current circumstances; I am the creator of them.
- There is only one source of all there is, and I am connected to that source by my thoughts and feelings.
- The universe wants and provides all I choose for myself without fail.

- I know that I have complete free will and that nothing can be done to me; it has to come through me.

When you believe these statements, your thoughts will automatically be about abundance, prosperity, and the knowledge of your unlimited creation potential.

Words

Now start speaking only those words that support your new beliefs. Avoid conversations that are all about drama, fear, and limiting beliefs. Open yourself only to those conversations that recognize your new truth. Since everything comes from the source of all there is, and you are now experiencing your connection to it, there can be no lack of what you want.

If you speak words of lack, the source will give you more lack. If you speak words of poverty, it will give you more poverty to speak about. If you speak words of abundance, joy, and happiness, it will give you more of those, too.

Actions

Live every moment as someone who knows the ultimate truth about how you can create the life experience you really want. Always act from a place of love, acceptance, and understanding because you now know that any resistance, regardless of what it's about, shuts down the flow between you and your source.

Let's take a simple example:

Choice . . .

Let's pretend you choose that a dollar will come into your experience today. You are clear on your choice—one dollar. You don't limit it to an actual dollar bill; you are open to that dollar coming in any form. This could be in the form of a coupon, or an overpaid bill, or a free cup of coffee for being such a good coffee-shop regular. Your job is to stay focused on the fact that a dollar will come into your experience today.

Thoughts . . .

You think thoughts of prosperity today. You imagine money pouring into your experience from all over the place. You think thoughts of abundance, and you know that you are entitled to that abundance.

Words . . .

You speak like someone who had a dollar show up today. You speak like you are the powerful creator you really are. You speak positive words that support your ability to create what you want. You use your words to support others in their creations as well.

Actions . . .

You move through your day as though the dollar has already come into your experience. You actually spend an extra dollar on something today.

You never doubt that a dollar will come into your experience because in your thoughts, words, and actions, you have already received the extra dollar. It has already been done; in your mind you have already experienced the dollar, so you no longer have to wait for anything. Being the person who already has the dollar is your attracting power.

This is how to live a life without expectation. How great would it be to live as though everything you chose to experience were already done?

I didn't have an example when I was writing this, so I put my attention on the thing I wanted—to have for my readers a great, undeniably clear example of how this works. Then I put my attention on what I really wanted, which was the feeling of accomplishment and satisfaction that I was doing a good job for my readers. I felt satisfied and accomplished, and had thoughts, spoke words, and took actions as though I already had my example written in my book. Then I let go, and this is what happened. A couple of hours later, I was on a book conference call with a great organization called Inspired U (www.inspireduniversity.com). During the call, Robert told us about his past sales experience. He would push and push, call and call, to get people to buy his products, in order to get more of what he thought he wanted—money. When he got tired of this approach (which was not working for him at all), it became clear to him that it was more important to be the person who already had the money so he didn't have to push anymore. He replaced his thoughts of scarcity with thoughts of abundance. He envisioned clients pouring into his experience; he chose to have them call him. He became the person who already had a thriving business, and that is exactly what he got! His phone started ringing. People started sending him and his company tens of thousands of dollars every week!

Robert understood that he had already had all that he wanted within him at every moment. He didn't really need the money to feel what he wanted to feel. Once he recognized that, he was able to attract more of those feelings by creating the things that he chose to amplify those feelings—like more money.

When Robert chose to think, feel, and act on his want, he allowed the results he wanted to pour in. By putting my attention on the same thing, in just a few short hours, the story I wanted for my book came into my physical experience!

Creating Powerful Thoughts, Words, and Actions

But, can't, have to, should. How do those words make you feel? Not so great, huh? How often do you use them? I invite you to take one of these words and count how many times you not only say it, but also how many times you think it in just one day. Chances are, it will be a lot!

I've been paying attention to using positive replacements for these words, but truth be told, they do come out every once in a while anyway. I hear them when I speak with my daughter. She'll ask if I can play with her, and sometimes I'll say, "I have to do the dishes." Ugh! That's not what I want my daughter to hear! Recently, I've been changing the words I use. Now I say, "I'll play with you in a minute; first I will finish the dishes." When she asks, "Mama, can we buy this?" instead of saying, "We don't have the money," which really isn't true, I will say, "I'm not going to spend my money on that today. Maybe another day, cutie pie."

We can't escape it. Words have emotional charge, whether we think them or say them out loud. Read this list and pay close attention to what happens to you physically when you simply think these words:

- I can't.
- I have to.
- I need to.
- I should.
- I won't.

    And now . . .

- I can.
- I want to.
- I choose to.
- I will.

Big difference, right? Today, pay attention to how many times you not only think but actually say these words. Notice what happens to you physically and emotionally when you use them.

Julia did this for a week, and she not only noticed her use of the negative words, but also how many people around her used them frequently, too. If you find that the people around you use lots of these words, you have a good indication of how much you use these words, too. Remember, like attracts like.

If you are prone to using negative phrasing more than positive, your attention is on what you don't want and you are not connected to your creation partner. On the other hand, if you find that you use the positive phrases more, then you are consciously connected and creating in the direction that you want.

So, how do you change your phrasing? It is just as easy as changing a "don't want" into a "do want."

Typically, unless you are highly emotionally charged, you think about what you are going to say before you actually say it. The important thing here is to be conscious not only about your thoughts and what you are about to say, but also about how you feel.

Take "but," for example. This word alone is responsible for squelching millions of dreams for people. Here are a few examples of dream killers:

- "I would love to do that for work, but blah, blah, blah."
- "That sounds like fun, but blah, blah, blah."
- "I wish I could, but blah, blah, blah."

Be honest—how many times have you said or thought something like this? Truth is, most things that follow a "but" are the product of ignorance driven by fear.

Here's another example:

- "So what do you really want to be doing for work?"
- "I would love to teach kids how to swim, but I can't make any money doing that."
- "Teaching kids to swim sounds great. How much money can you make doing that?"
- "I don't know."
- "Oh, you just said that you couldn't make any money doing that."
- "I'm sure it can't pay me enough to live on."
- "You're sure, but you don't know?"

Did you notice how quickly the dream got squelched? Did you notice that the one word that got it on the path to destruction was that little three-letter word "but"? It doesn't matter if in reality there is a high-paying swim instructor job out there. The fact is that because my client "thinks" there isn't, her truth is her truth, so there isn't one for *her*. It's simple, yet powerful. You may start out being positive, "I would love to . . ." and then you knock it out into the field of dead dreams as soon as you think or say the word "but."

Okay, I think you get it now . . . NO MORE "BUTS"! The next time you want to use the word "but"—maybe you were feeling great about something, and then you felt the need to end that feel-good moment—replace it in the nick of time with a sturdy "I choose to . . ."

For example, "I want to own my own business, but I don't have the money to finance it" becomes "I want to own my own business. I choose to find ways that I can finance it."

See how simple that is? When you use the word "but," you have built a brick wall. When you use the phrase, "I choose to," you are creating a great next step on which to put your attention.

Not bad, right? Let's try a couple more . . .

"I want to find work I love, but I'm sure it doesn't pay that much" becomes "I want to find work I love. I choose to find a way to earn enough money doing work I love."

"I want to find my ideal partner, but we always have to settle for something" becomes "I want to find my ideal partner. I choose to understand who my ideal partner is and then put my attention on being that way myself so that I can attract this person easily."

Take a moment to write down all of the dreams that you have killed with a "but." This is a great start to your "do want" list. Revive these ideas; they came to you for a reason. Allow the old, crumpled dreams to come back to life, turn them into "do wants," and see how far you choose to go with them.

Listen to how others kill their dreams, and know that you are now choosing to be the person who lives your dreams!

Another dream-killing phrase is "What if . . ." I worked with a CEO once who made this simple for me. Someone said, "What if we fail?" and the CEO said, without a blink, "What if we are wildly successful?"

Again, you don't want to fail, so flip it to what you really want.

"What if we run out of money?" becomes "What if the money consistently pours in?"

"What if I can't find a job I love?" becomes "What if I find a job that exceeds my expectations?"

"What if I never find my ideal partner?" becomes "What if when I find my ideal partner, that person is even better than I imagined?"

The goal with the words you think and use is to go from a feeling place of need to choosing a want. When we create, we are really just choosing. Using words that support what we are being—conscious creators—keeps us on track and lets our creative partner know that we are serious, not wishy-washy. We become magnets for what we are saying we want!

Pay attention to the conversations and experiences you get involved in.

- If you have chosen for income to pour into your experience now, you probably won't want to spend time around the water cooler talking about how bad the economy is.

- If you have chosen that more clients will come into your experience effortlessly, you don't want to spend time complaining about how your industry is in a downturn.

- If you have chosen to be with your ideal partner, you don't want to spend time complaining that you're too old to find love.

- If you want to be healthy, the last thing you want to do is turn on the surgery channel.

- If you have chosen to experience peace and harmony in your life, please turn off the news!

What you expose yourself to is your choice. It is also where a lot of your thoughts and words come from. Simplify your creation by choosing to experience events that give you the same feelings you are intending to have when you have what you want.

Now, thinking and speaking like something is there when we can't see it is one thing, but acting like it? How do we do that? This is where the rubber hits the road, so to speak. How do we act like persons who have what we want, when we don't actually have what we want in front of us? How do we drive the car if it is not sitting in our driveway? How do we spend the money when it is not sitting in our bank account? How do we act like we are in a relationship when there's no one there?

Again, it is the feeling that's important, so take actions that people would take who already have what they want. I think the best way to help you understand this one is to demonstrate it through my personal experience.

As I mentioned before, my financial affairs had hit the skids over the past two years. It all came to a head just around the time I got this book deal. Creditors were calling, and foreclosure notices and letters from lawyers were coming in the mail.

It got to the point where I would turn off the ringer on the phone and refuse to get the mail. I felt fear every time I was driving and an electric company van would pass by. I felt sick every time a gas company truck came down my street because I thought they were coming to turn off my heat. I really thought someone was going to come to my door and take me to jail! Ugly, I know, but true.

Guess what thoughts I was thinking during this time? *I have no money. All I get in the mail are more bills. I have no income coming in. I can't believe I let this happen.* Of course, I kept getting more of the same.

My conversations with my partner were all about how we didn't have any money. "We can't spend money on that." "How else can we limit our spending?" Of course, we kept getting more of the same.

For a long time, I just tried to ignore it all. Then one day, I made a clear and conscious choice: I recognized that if I had done such an amazing job of creating this mess, then I could now simply choose to create something else. I chose to experience my bills being paid in full and on time. Really, it was that simple. What made it powerful was that I chose to get conscious and start thinking, speaking, and acting like someone whose bills were paid in full and on time.

One day, I was reading *The Wizard of Oz* to my daughter, and we came to the part where Dorothy throws the water on the witch, and she melts into nothing. Well, as we say in Massachusetts, at that moment "light dawned on Marblehead," and I decided to take some inspired action.

First, I called all my creditors to arrange payments. Now, I still didn't have the money, but I knew it would be there when the payments were due. I made arrangements to get the mortgage back up to date, and I made sure that all of the utilities were taken care of so I didn't have to fear that my lights and heat would be turned off.

I turned on the heat even though I had a twinge that I might not have the money when the bill came in. I ignored that twinge, turned up the heat, and was consistently rewarded by my creation partner with the money to pay the bill!

My witch melted away! I started thinking thoughts about abundance and prosperity. My conversations were about having plenty of money, and clients started to pour in. I was grateful every time I had money to spend. I became the person whose bills were paid in full and on time, and guess what? They have been ever since!

Being a person who already has what you've chosen to experience is what eliminates the one thing that will slow down your creation—negative feelings about what you've chosen to create! If it's already done, how could there be anything more to doubt or be negative about?

Easier said than done? Yep, but the more you practice being conscious, the more you will allow this whole process of creation to become second nature.

Before we move on to overcoming some common

creation obstacles, let's review where you are with your unfulfilled intention:

- You've been affirming your new Creation Foundation Beliefs.
- You are keeping clear on your intention, or what you've chosen to experience by enjoying your script out loud.
- You have identified and started invoking the feelings you desire to feel.
- You have written and affirmed your being script.

Overcoming Obstacles to Allowing

You're "buzzing" along, feeling amazing, being grateful, enjoying your creation roller-coaster ride when all of a sudden, BOOM, something happens—you didn't get the promotion, the deal fell through, the partner of your dreams didn't call. Now you've not only stopped "buzzing," but you've started plummeting down the "it will never come" spiral.

This is where readers of *Excuse Me* have said, "Excuse me, but it is really hard to stay consistent when things like this happen!" I know, and that is why we are going to spend some time on how to keep the "buzz on," no matter what's happening on your roller coaster.

So let's take a closer look. Notice what happened: you were fine, something happened, and you were not so fine. Most of us think the "something" that happened is what threw us down the spiral. Nope! It was our reaction to the "something" that knocked us for a loop.

Being a powerful allower is all about being in alignment with what you want through your thoughts, words, and actions. So ask yourself, "Would people who already have what they wanted ever think they wouldn't get what they want?" No, because they already have it!

If you are being the person who already has the ideal relationship, and the person you liked didn't call, it really wouldn't matter because you'd know that *everything is unfolding perfectly*. In your mind's eye, you are already enjoying the relationship!

So, powerful allowers . . .

- know that once they have determined what they want, it is already created, and they are simply responsible for keeping their attention on it and taking inspired action toward it. There is nothing to worry about.

- know that this creation process never fails, and that they are masters at using its principles.

- know that it is natural for them to allow and not force their circumstances.

When circumstances happen that don't seem to be in alignment with what we have chosen to create, our first reaction is often to put our attention on what we don't want—the fact that our creation is not here yet. Immediately, we start creating in the opposite direction, thereby slowing down the reality of what we have chosen. Then we start to question these principles, and we really start to feel that we aren't capable of applying them consistently. Then it is all over until we can pick ourselves back up again and remember that life is right now, and we are supposed to be enjoying it!

Many people have expressed the concern that if they have one negative thought, it will cancel their creation. Well, since it is always about what you think and feel, if you think you've canceled your creation with one negative thought, then you have. But if you had a negative thought, but you believe that since you are consciously shifting your attention back to what you have chosen it will still come, then come it will!

What is happening here is that you are judging your circumstances, and that judgment is causing you fear, doubt, and worry. On top of this, you may also be personalizing these circumstances, thereby making the emotional impact of the situation a hundred times worse.

Managing our thoughts becomes impossible when we choose to personalize events and circumstances around us. Think about it . . . whenever you react to something that has happened, you are coming from a place of judgment, and typically that judgment is about you. This is what personalization really is: it's a judgment about something else that, if taken a bit deeper, is a judgment you have about yourself. How many times have you judged another person, only to admit to yourself later that you were really judging yourself?

Every time we personalize, we jeopardize being open to the flow of receiving what we have chosen to create. It is one of the worst forms of resistance because it can send us into a self-judgment frenzy. The bottom line is that judgment kills joy! Here you are, "buzzing" along, enjoying the ride, then something happens, you judge it as "bad," and you are no longer enjoying the ride. You have successfully killed your joy! The fact is that "somethings" are happening all the time around us—some we feel are good; some we feel are bad. But if we felt that all "somethings" were just as they should be, we would continue to enjoy our ride!

The goal is not to get off the roller coaster, but learn how to take the fast, winding ride while keeping your reactions conscious and centered. This will allow your creations to unfold beautifully.

Shakespeare got it right when he said, "There is no good or bad; only thinking makes it so." Here's a way to react to the current situation in a way that keeps fear, doubt, and worry out of your way so that you can be the allower that you really are. Say to yourself, *It is what it is!* That's it? Yes! *It is what it is!*

Once you are able to take the emotion out of the equation, you can call on your new beliefs to take you to the next level. You can't know how your creation partner is going to bring your chosen experience into life, so you just have to believe: *My creation partner provides what I choose for myself without fail!* So therefore, *everything is unfolding perfectly now!*

You now know that when things don't seem to be working out, your creation is still on the way—it will just be bigger or better than you expected at first. When Julie Andrews lost to Audrey Hepburn the part of Eliza Doolittle for the movie of *My Fair Lady,* she thought she'd been dealt a blow, but *The Sound of Music* was right around the corner!

Now you can consciously choose to put your attention back on being the person who already has what you have chosen to experience through your thoughts, words, and actions. You are allowing again!

This will work, but it may take some practice to get there. Lynn offered a couple of great tricks to "switch focus" that we will review in a moment. Readers of *Excuse Me* loved the switch tricks, but they sometimes had trouble dealing with the emotions that arose when things didn't seem to be going their way. When you are having emotions about a particular unwanted situation, the first step is to accept that you are experiencing fear, doubt, and worry. Part of the problem when we judge and personalize circumstances is that we get frustrated that we are somehow doing this creation thing wrong. We start beating ourselves up for not being consistent. Hence the spiral!

You may have heard it before, but what you resist

persists. If you choose to put attention on the fact that you are failing, what will you attract? More failure. By resisting, you are attracting the very thing you don't want.

Instead, if you simply accept that you are feeling these feelings, you can get your attention back on what you have chosen to experience. When you accept, you can choose another course.

Lynn says, "There is only one way to stop the messes in our lives from getting worse: stop focusing on them. If we can accept—from the depths of our being—that our problems are not caused by our boss, our mate, our raucous kids, the IRS, or the drunk on the freeway, then we have a chance to wipe those problems away in the same way we attracted them: by our energy flow. Only this time, through a significantly different vibration."

Feel the power of your new belief: I am not my current circumstances; I am the sole creator of them.

Accept, even bless, the mess you have created, and choose to create something else! Now you are open to understanding why you fall into these spirals so that you can create yourself as a person who accepts all circumstances and events as stepping stones to what you have chosen to experience!

Understanding Your Victim
Modus Operandi (MO)

I wanted to experience a fire walk, a personal-development event where you walk across hot coals (www.openflame.biz). Since there were none of these events happening in my area, I was going to have to host it if I wanted to experience one. Not a big deal? I'm a creator, so this should be a cinch, right?

So I set my intention and started taking inspired action. Now if I were a true creator, I would have had no worries about how this was all going to turn out, but I did have one important worry. I had to have at least ten paid participants in order to be able to pay the fire-walking instructor. If I didn't get the ten, I would have to pay the difference: $150 per person.

Okay, I'm a creator, I thought. *I'll just put my attention on having more than enough participants, and they will come.* So I did, and they started coming. Little by little, the numbers started to increase. Then it happened. Three days before, I was still down by two people, and I got an e-mail saying that two people had to cancel. Now I was down four people with only four days left.

This is where my Victim MO kicked in—the typical way I always thought when things went wrong. I knew this was going to happen. What am I going to do? I'm going to have to come up with $750 to pay the instructor. I should never have taken this on. What was I thinking? Everything I do never works out the way I want it to. This creation stuff doesn't work. It is never enough!

There I was, so far from being a creator. I let my Victim MO surface and take over the situation. I was not committed to being a creator at that moment. I was committed to falling into my comfortable victim role.

As always, I had a choice: I could get back to being a creator, or I could be a victim. Once I realized what I had done, I chose to get back into my creator self and refocus my attention on my original intention—that I would have more than enough participants to pay the instructor.

What a relief that was! Then I got an e-mail saying that someone else wanted to register. Instead of saying to myself, *I still have three to go,* I chose to say, *Only three to go!* Much more like my creator self. The night before, one more person called to register. Only two to go. Now the pressure was on. I needed two more people, and it was the day of the event.

The morning of the event, as I was sitting on my couch thinking, *They will come,* the phone rang. Someone who had already registered asked if she could bring a friend. Only one to go.

It was the beginning of the event. Folks were starting to show up. I was still down one person when someone who had registered way in the beginning showed up. I had forgotten that this person was coming. There was my tenth!

The conscious choice is ours. Do we remain creators, or do we become victims? We know when it begins—we start to feel badly about what we say we want. It is in that moment that we can choose to enjoy the ride, or to hold on for dear life. The results always indicate what we choose!

What is your Victim MO? Are you prone to saying things like:

"This always happens to me."

"Nothing ever goes the way I plan."

"This creation stuff doesn't work."

All this is just a warning that you are not allowing your creation partner to work through you because these thoughts don't feel good. Now that you are conscious of what you are doing, you can choose to be your Creator MO by using the Four Steps of Creation:

1. Don't want—to be a victim.
2. Do want—to be a powerful creator.
3. Feel—I am so happy and grateful now that I am a powerful creator working with my creation partner who creates with me what I choose without fail.
4. Allow—I am now being the person who accepts what I'm feeling and chooses to put my attention back on being grateful for the fact that I already have all that I have chosen.

With my new Creator MO, when things come up that could be perceived as negative, I can now say things like:

"My good always comes to me."

"Everything is unfolding perfectly."

"I am a master creator."

So how do you manage your Victim MO? Accept that you are experiencing it, and get the emotion out of the equation by being the feeling that you are having.

Be Your Emotion

The technique of being an emotion came to me one night while putting my daughter to bed. Typically, I sit with her while she starts to fall asleep. Because it's quiet and dark, I often focus on what happened that day.

One night while thinking about my day, I became frustrated about something that had happened. As soon as I started feeling frustrated, the cycle started. I thought about why I was frustrated, then I felt frustrated, then I had another thought about why I was frustrated, then I felt even more frustrated. I bet you know what I'm talking about here!

All of a sudden, I have no idea why, I heard myself say, "Just be frustration." As soon as I said it, the feeling disappeared! It was amazing; it vanished, leaving my mind and body free of the negative feelings. Then I was able to look at the circumstances and see that they weren't at all as bad as I thought. I was free!

Thoughts and emotions feed off each other. You know the cycle: you have a not-so-pleasant thought, and then you feel the feeling of the thought, which makes you think more unpleasant thoughts. And so the downward spiral begins. We have all been there, and so we can recognize the power of this cycle!

I invite you to stop the cycle by just being the emotion you are feeling. Simply BE it. Now, I am not talking about acting out the emotion. Being angry is not the same as acting angry by picking up plates and throwing them across the kitchen. Being sad is not crying in the bathroom with a box of tissues. To be an emotion, simply say that you are that emotion.

In those moments, just say to yourself . . .

- Be anger!
- Be frustration!
- Be sadness!
- Be fear!
- Be confusion!
- Be the noun, not the verb!

The goal is to separate the feeling from the thought so that they can't feed off each other. Your feelings can't survive without your thoughts, and your thoughts can't get worse without your feelings.

Once you are the negative emotion that you are feeling, it will vanish and leave you with the thought that caused it in the first place. When you've unharnessed the thought and the emotion, you are better able to deal with the real truth of the thought. The cycle is broken, and the road is open to make a conscious choice about where you want to put your attention next.

Let's say you are driving along with your intention being that you want to have a peaceful day. Someone cuts you off in traffic. Your immediate reaction is anger, followed by the thought, *What a jerk!* This is followed by more anger, followed by, *Here I was trying to have a nice day, and I get cut off!* This is followed by still more anger, *It is too hard to stay positive when there are jerks like that out here . . .* The cycle begins!

In that moment, stop and say, "Just BE anger." Watch how the feeling of anger disappears. Now you can put your attention back on having a peaceful day.

You may be saying, "Huh?" Many of my clients say that at first, and then they try it and can't believe how well it works. Here's why it works. Ever notice a storm in nature? Storms are typically short and powerful. And once their energy is spent, they simply disappear. On the flip side, we usually have relatively stable weather for extended periods of time.

It's the same thing with negative and positive feelings. The negative ones only stay as long as we give them energy by feeding and amplifying them with our thoughts, while the positive ones seem to last naturally. This is an indication that we are meant to have long-lasting positive feelings.

At our very core, we are all emotions—positive and negative. When we choose to experience anger, frustration, or sadness, they don't feel so good, so they don't last very long. Truly, we are made of pure positive emotions—love, acceptance, and gratitude—and as long as we choose what we are experiencing, these positive emotions last forever.

If I were to say to you right now, "Be happiness," you could immediately connect with the word "happiness" and feel happiness. If I were to say to you, "Be angry," as in the technique described above, you would not be able to conjure it up on the spot without a trigger, and therefore you wouldn't really feel angry.

Why do you think positive feelings feel good? Because we are them! That's why we connect with them just by saying a positive word.

Using this technique will separate you from the cycle of negative thoughts and emotions so that you can get your focus back on what you already have. Now you've opened the door to greater success with switching focus.

Switching Focus

According to Lynn, "You don't have to change it (your perceived problem); you just have to stop focusing on it!" Let's review two of Lynn's switch tricks:

"Trick #1. Switch focus. Now!"

Lynn invites you to change your focus to anything that feels good. Anything! The goal is to change your energy, even if only a little bit. Find something you enjoy and put your attention on it. Lynn suggests focusing on "your mate (if you've got a great relationship), your home, a song, your doggie, your new sweatshirt, a chocolate sundae, making love, your upcoming vacation, your last vacation, a special restaurant, your youngster asleep."

Now that you have eliminated the negative feeling, and your attention is on things that make you feel good, you can shift your attention back onto your want and away from your unwanted condition. Lynn suggests talking out loud about what you want.

State your powerful, positive intention, which should bring your script to mind as well. Congratulations! Now you are consciously shifting away from your unwanted condition and back to your chosen experience!

"Trick #4. Do something fun. Now!"

Lynn advises, "Get physical! Go for a walk, polish your car, brush your cat, buy a new suit, bake a cake, play poker, trim your flowers, go to a movie, whatever turns you on that will take your stuck focus off the condition and soften your resistance to flowing the higher energy. Once you feel the shift happen, start talking out loud, gently at first, about what you want in place of the unwanted condition."

Getting physical is a great way to release negative energy from your body. The next time you are feeling negative, pay attention to how your body is responding. When I am not flying particularly high with positive emotion, my daughter will look at me and ask, "Mama, why does your face look like this?" and she'll look at me with a furrowed brow and scrunched-up eyes. I didn't even realize that that was how I looked!

There is an amazing sense of release when we relax our bodies and let the negative energy flow out of us. It not only clears our bodies, but it clears our minds as well. We are reconnected to our creation partner, and we can now enjoy the ride again.

So, accepting that you are experiencing fear, doubt, and worry, knowing that everything is unfolding perfectly now, moving beyond the negative emotion, and switching your focus back onto what you have chosen to experience is your key to actually enjoying the ups and downs of your creation roller coaster. Here's how Susan was able to switch focus to get what she wanted:

Susan, a real-estate agent, had been very worried about money. She believed that the real-estate market had dried up, and for her it had. She wasn't getting any listings, and the listings she had weren't selling. She was filled with fear about how the bills were going to get paid, and she didn't know where her next dollar was going to come from.

Then Susan chose to switch her thoughts and feelings from her unfulfilled condition to knowing that money was now starting to flow in. Her bills would be paid, and her financial picture would turn around.

When the bills came in, she was grateful that they were already paid, even though she didn't know how that would happen. When she had to spend money, she was grateful that she had the money to spend. When an unexpected expense came up, she knew it was all unfolding perfectly.

Here are two e-mails I received from her.

E-mail one:

"Yesterday, my car had to go into the shop, so I was driving my partner's car. I had $690 in the bank. Nissan repair was $232. Then, as we were driving to the shop to pick up the Nissan, the Subaru made a loud clunking noise every time I braked. It just started on the way to the garage. Got there, picked up the Nissan, but dropped off the Outback for exploratory surgery. I talked to the mechanic—the car needs new front brakes, rotors, and a slider. Cost: $455. New account balance: $3. And I'm totally relaxed and happy that we have the money."

E-mail two:

"and a $1,000 check just arrived in the mail . . ."

Susan knew everything would work out, she was being "totally relaxed and happy that we have the money," and the money came. Susan left the door open for it to flow in because she was being the person who allowed it to flow in. She was relaxed and enjoying her ride!

Universal 2x4s

How many times have you had a hunch and ignored it? How many times has your gut said to go a certain way and you rejected it? How many times have you had a thought that felt soooooo good, and you followed it with the word "but"?

Being a powerful allower means listening, and listening means paying attention to the signs that your creation partner is giving you the experiences you have chosen. Remember, your creation partner can't do anything to you, only *through* you, so you have to pay attention and take inspired action.

Universal 2x4s are little bits of guidance (and even objects) that we need to make our intentions transpire. They are dropped, sometimes unceremoniously and sometimes very dramatically, into our laps courtesy of our very own creation partner. I call them 2x4s because when they arrive, it sometimes it feels as if we've been hit by one.

They go something like this . . .

- Robert was on a call, and the person he was talking to mentioned reading *Excuse Me*. Robert was half paying attention because he was checking his e-mail. As he was reading, a new e-mail popped into his inbox. The subject line said, "Read *Excuse Me, Your Life Is Waiting*."

- One day, Jan hopped onto the Hampton Roads Publishing Web site to get their address to send them a book proposal. The same day she received an e-mail from me requesting a story for my book because I had seen her review of *Excuse Me* on Amazon that day.

- I had a great idea to do a talk. I rented out a fantastic space and advertised it. It cost about $500 at a time when I really didn't have $500 to spare. No one showed up! As I was in tears, literally asking if I should give this all up, I heard a *whoosh* right over my head. A hawk landed squarely on the roof in front of me, about five feet above. He was facing forward, away from me. I was paralyzed. I didn't know if this was going to be one of the greatest moments of my life, or, if he chose to attack me, one of the worst. I stood there in awe. Then he turned his head, looked directly into my eyes for what seemed like an eternity, and then flew off. I took it as a sign to keep moving forward no matter what my current circumstances.

- I was very upset about something, and I could feel the panic growing. At that moment, I looked at my inbox and got an e-mail with the subject line, "Don't Panic!"

In 1990, Connie was trying to decide if she should go to Romania to adopt a little girl. She writes:

I was afraid because I don't like flying, and I would have to go alone. I didn't know anyone there, and it seemed like an impossible task. I was in the Barnes & Noble bookstore looking for something to read when, suddenly, a book fell off the shelf. I put it back and walked up the aisle. It fell off again. I thought, *That's odd.* I returned it once more, very securely. As I turned, it fell off again! I said, "Okay, I'll buy it." The book was *Three Magic Words,* by U. S. Andersen. The book inspired me to go forward. I referred to it constantly while in Romania. It took me 22 months to adopt my little girl. I faced many harrowing experiences, including looking down the barrels of rifles as soldiers stormed out of the back of a truck toward me and having drunk minors threaten to club us and burn our car. In the past 16 years, I have had three books that I read so much and so thoroughly that they fell apart and had to be replaced. *Three Magic Words* was one of those. I've also read Lynn Grabhorn's books many times. Both have helped me through enormously difficult times as an adoptive parent of two children with severe challenges. We were told our son was too brain-damaged to ever learn to read. In seventh grade, he had a first-grade reading level. We did not give up. We got him the services he needed and even sold our house to help pay for them. He went from a first- to a 12th-grade reading level in two and a half years. He went back to public school and took

Honors English, Honors Physics, and Honors Algebra 2. He has since finished a year in college. My daughter has also overcome incredible challenges. Without the emotional support of these two books, I would never have been able to survive.

Connie's book had to fall off the shelf three times before she recognized that she had been hit by a 2x4, and she should buy the book! Sometimes the delivery is exactly what we asked for, and sometimes it's not as crystal-clear as "looking down the barrels of rifles." Bottom line, it's an indication that when we set our intention, and if we simply pay attention, we are ultimately guided.

These occurrences are also known as synchronicities. Whatever we choose to call them, the important thing is that we recognize them as evidence that we are always supported in our *true* desires. And when I say true, I mean true to you!

What is great about your creation partner is that it will keep delivering the signs even when you are not paying close attention. It will keep delivering until we finally get it! It helps to think of them as 2x4s in order to understand the tremendous power and support being delivered.

I thought of the term "universal 2x4" because of my client Carolyn F. Carolyn is an amazing creator. She will literally declare her intention, and a sign of support will show up for her almost immediately.

Carolyn's first known experience with a universal 2x4 came after she did a visualization in a class I taught. The visualization asked folks to go five years into the future to meet their Higher Selves and ask them questions.

Carolyn is like a lot of us for two reasons. First, she was unhappy at work. She was a director of a Meals on Wheels program, but she wanted to find work that she was more passionate about. Second, even though she thought she didn't know what she wanted, deep down she did know. She just couldn't be honest about it.

The class was instructed to arrive at a place where they would meet their Higher Selves. Carolyn landed at a farm in the mountains. At this farm, she saw a ring with horses and disabled children. She saw how the horses and the children were working together. It was clear that this was an animal-assisted therapy farm where disabled children were interacting with animals as part of their rehabilitation.

Carolyn noticed a man working with the children. He was someone she had known in the past and hadn't heard from in over five years. He was apparently the owner of the farm.

Carolyn went on to meet her Higher Self and asked her many questions. She came out of the visualization a bit confused, not so much by the farm or the disabled children—because deep down inside she knew that she would like to pursue this idea—but more because of the friend she had seen.

The next class Carolyn told us that when she got home the night after the visualization class, she checked her phone and there was a message from that very same friend. Again, she hadn't heard from him in five years!

Soon after, Carolyn and I started working together on getting her clear on what she really wanted to be doing for work. You would think that after an experience like the one described above that Carolyn would be all set and start at least exploring the direction her visualization suggested. Nope, Carolyn needed a couple more 2x4s.

Once she understood that she really wanted to work with service dogs, the 2x4s started rolling in.

• Every week she saw at least one service dog. How many do you see in a month?

- When she was away on business, she picked up a magazine in the airport and opened it randomly to an article about rescue dogs.

- She received an unsolicited flyer asking for volunteers to train service puppies at a local prison.

It would seem that Carolyn had it easy. After all, she visualized what she was interested in, and then all these opportunities to pursue it kept coming into her experience. But Carolyn is like a lot of us who get a glimmer of what we want, but choose instead to put our attention on thinking about all the reasons why we shouldn't pursue it.

It took Carolyn three years, but she recently left her job, packed up her home and her dog, Aspen, and is off to California to study Assisted Dog Training. What happens after graduation? Carolyn is not so sure, but she knows that all she has to do is set her intention and look around to know what steps she will take next.

How many times have you been hit by a universal 2x4 and done nothing about it? Count the number of times you've said, "It would be great if . . ." and then just left it at that. If you had a crystal ball and looked back on those times with your full attention, I bet you would see how there were signs of support, but you just didn't acknowledge them because your attention was on not having what you said you wanted.

The best way to listen to your creation partner is to simply accept what is, knowing that you have done your job of setting your intention and keeping your thoughts and feelings on it, while allowing your creation partner to work through you. Seeing all circumstances as opportunities for the experience you have chosen is what allows it to come through you. Staying connected to your creation partner through positive feelings will determine the speed at which you will receive what you have chosen to experience.

I meet a lot of people these days who are interested in these principles, but it's usually by phone or e-mail. So, I set an intention that I wanted to start meeting folks face to face. I did my job, set my intention, created a script of how I would feel once I was experiencing what I had chosen, and then put my attention on being those feelings today while allowing my creation partner to create the people, circumstances, and events.

One day, I was putting my daughter down for her nap. It was one of those days when I wanted to get a bunch of work done while she was asleep. Well, she decided that she didn't want to take a nap. In the past, I would have been frustrated—not with her, but with the fact that I wouldn't be able to get my work done. That day, I decided to simply accept what was—she wasn't going down, and I wasn't going to get that extra hour of work done. I decided that everything was unfolding perfectly.

Sammi got up, got dressed, and we jumped in the car to go to the post office. I had planned to go to the post office that day, but if Sammi had napped, we would have gone later. While we were standing in line, I noticed that the woman in line behind me was holding the book, *Ask and It Is Given,* by Esther and Jerry Hicks. Not only did she have that book, but she was also holding the movie, *What the "Bleep" Do We Know!?* As you may know, these two items indicate that the person holding them is very into creation principles.

This was one of those times that you just say, "Okay, I get it now! All I have to do is keep my good vibrations up, and you bring me all that I choose!" I struck up a conversation with this woman, and we are going to get in touch toward the end of the summer.

My intention was fulfilled because I knew that there

was no reason to be frustrated, it would all work out, and it did! I stayed connected to my creation partner and ended up in exactly the right place at the right time.

So let go, feel good, know that is all working out perfectly, and see how magical your life becomes when you become a great allower!

And, Finally, Here It Comes, There It Goes

Olivia wrote a letter to me about a recent experience she had with creating.

Dear Doreen:
There are a lot of things I want to share with you about the results I've gotten with the manifesting tools in Lynn's book. One of them is that I visualized or made a "script" about a certain person I wanted to have in my life. I was feeling very lonely and sad, and was having problems in my relationship, but I was afraid to break up with my boyfriend.

So I decided to write what I wanted exactly in a new partner and started visualizing every day. At first, it was a little difficult, but I felt so good while I was visualizing that it became easier. Time passed. After about a month and a half, I was living more in the imagined reality than in my "real" relationship, and that's when things started to move.

A friend sent me to a Web page link for a dating site and suggested that I sign up, just to see if I could meet someone I liked. I felt that it was a clue to finding the person I was looking for, and so I entered my profile and a picture. The next day, a man—who had all of the attributes I was looking for—wrote to me. The list of attributes I'd requested included that he be British, rich, handsome, never married, wanting to get married, with no children, etc. Well, this guy was just exactly what I wanted!!! And he invited me out. He was calling me like crazy and sending e-mails every day.

The sad thing is that I screwed up my manifestation with doubts. I was still dating my boyfriend (with whom I was having problems), but he started acting more loving, generous, and romantic, so I felt quite badly about searching for someone else.

Several days later, I fell into a low-frequency mood, and the new guy stopped calling!

Notice what Olivia did: she got clear on what she wanted next, felt great about it, and started seeing results. But in the end, she put the brakes on her creation partner because she wasn't being the person who was in a new relationship. She was being the person in her old relationship, feeling badly about wanting a new one.

Now that Olivia is conscious, she can go back to her original intention and see if it is something she really wants. Maybe she really wants a better relationship with her current boyfriend—she'll have to decide. What's important is that she got conscious and can now choose to create in a new direction!

So if you put the brakes on, rethink so that you can re-create!

The exercise we have gone through—taking your unfulfilled intention and you through the creation process—was designed so that you don't have to put the brakes on your creation partner like Olivia did. You are now conscious, clear, focused, being, and allowing of the process. So throw your hands in the air! You don't have to hold on anymore because you now have the tools to enjoy your creation roller-coaster ride—not later, not next year, not when everything you want is done and dusted, but right now!

Creation Principles Really Work!

Jay was having trouble getting honest about what she really wanted to do for a living. She thought she wanted to do all sorts of things that would bring her enough money so she could do what she really wanted to do. Then she realized she had all of her attention on the "how" rather than on what she really wanted. She decided to take her attention off the "how" and put it on her real want: to create theatrical performances on radio. She wrote out her script, got into the feeling place of it, and committed to not thinking about how this might happen—especially since she knew no one in the radio industry! That same week, Jay received an instant message from someone she didn't know. Instead of ignoring it, she was inspired to write back and let the sender know she must have received the message by mistake. She received a reply back and started a conversation. You guessed it . . . it turned out the person worked in radio and knew a lot of people who could help Jay with her project!

FIVE

Excuse Me, Your Ideal Life, Health, Wealth, Romance, and Work Are NOW

> You never again have to be afraid of "them"
> or "it," no matter who or what they may be,
> unless you choose.
>
> —Lynn Grabhorn,
> *Excuse Me, Your Life Is Waiting*

You understand the laws . . .

- Like attracts like.
- What you put your thoughts and feelings on, you create.

You know your job . . .

- Be clear on what you want.
- Stay clear on what you want.
- Recognize and take action on the "how" that the universe delivers to you.

You have been through the process . . .

- Know what you don't want.
- Know what you do want.
- Feel it.
- Allow it to come.

You now know how to master allowing by being the person who already has what you have chosen to experience through your . . .

- thoughts.
- words.
- actions.

In sum, you have all the tools to be a master creator! So why does your life sometimes seem like a bowl of porridge, smooth in some respects, but a bit lumpy in others? Why is it that your relationship is steamy, but your finances are not? Or maybe you have fragile health, but you love your job to bits?

The reason for the inconsistency is that you carry different beliefs of what can and cannot be in each area of your life. That means that each area involves varying degrees of difficulty when it comes to creating what you want.

Let's do a little exercise. On a scale of 1 to 5—1 being the easiest and 5 being the most difficult—rate the following areas according to how easy you believe it would be to consciously create what you want:

- Health
- Wealth
- Romance and relationships
- Work

Right now, mine would look something like this,

- Health - 4
- Wealth - 5
- Romance and relationships - 2
- Work - 4

You can easily see the area that might be a little tougher for me. What about you? Which areas are scoring pretty low in the can-create matrix? Where do you have difficulty believing that you can consistently wield your new creative power?

Take the area that's lagging behind the rest and ask yourself the following questions:

- Are you completely honest with yourself and others about what you want in this area?
- Why don't you believe that you can create anything you want in this area?
- How much conscious attention do you currently put on creating in this area?

If you are experiencing some localized creation frustration, you can pretty much narrow it down to the following: you're probably not speaking your truth, you're indulging in some limiting beliefs, and you probably don't spend a lot of conscious, powerful, positive effort in this area—because you're afraid. All together, those things make it nearly impossible to create.

It is important to realize that you are actually in a living, evolving relationship with all of the areas of your life, including money, career, business, romance, and health. And, just like relationships with different people, each different area of your life is unique and provokes likewise unique reactions. In one or two categories, you may feel like a master. Other areas you may like, but not trust. And still others may provoke a passionate love/hate response.

So, let's dream. Just indulge me a little bit here. How would your various relationships with people change if you weren't needy at all, but simply chose to experience other people for who they were? Or what if you took a job because you wanted to experience doing a specific kind of work, not because you needed the paycheck or the prestige? Or let's say you made lots and lots of cash, not because you needed money to be happy, but because you just wanted to experience such wealth.

When you don't need something, it's more fun to create it, and it's more effective, too. Need is based on fear, and so it attracts more fear. Gratitude is based on love, and so it attracts more experiences for which to be grateful.

Spend a day trying to think of everything that comes into your life as a bonus, not a need. All of it is just something you have chosen to experience, including all those knotty "problems."

I did this exercise for one whole day recently, and now I'm trying to do it every day. The most profound shift came when I applied it to my daughter. Every time she said, "I love you the best, Mama," every time she wrapped her arms around my neck, every time she ran up and hugged my leg, I thought, *What a bonus!* I realized I didn't *need* love from my daughter. In fact, I didn't need anything from her. I just enjoyed her love.

Imagine if we thought of all our relationships in that way—not just the ones with people, but also the ones with the different aspects of our lives. If you want to break through your frustration, then create loving and accepting relationships with all of the areas of your life— health, wealth, romance and relationships, and work.

Remember: Be conscious to be consistent! By deciding to create powerful, positive relationships with each area of your life, you open the door to create all that you choose in those areas!

Your Ideal Life Is Now

What is the one thing that cuts across all areas of your life? You know the answer . . . YOU! You don't get up in the morning, unzip yourself, and march one half to work, while the other half stays home to rustle up a pot of tea and deal with your personal life.

Since you are the only constant variable in all areas of your life—financial, career, business, relationships, health, etc.—understanding what you want for your whole life experience is your foundation. If you don't know what you want your overall life experience to be, creating what you want in each area is disjointed and inefficient.

So I suggest that you forget about all of the fiddly details for a moment and start at the top. Determine what is important for you to experience at the highest level. All of the different areas are interconnected, and the balance between them will determine your choices in every area. For example, if spending time with your family (romance and relationships) and getting a lot of sleep (health) are important to you, you wouldn't want a job that required 60 percent travel (work).

What life experience do you choose to create from a high-altitude vantage point? Is it one filled with joy, family, harmony, peace, and excitement? And if so, what do those words really mean to you? Define them!

Create a life intention script that demonstrates all of the qualities you desire. Here's an example: "I am so happy and grateful now that I am living a life filled with joy, peace, harmony, and excitement. My days are now filled with only those things that I choose to create for myself. I have plenty of time to do all that I choose to do and love that I am so close and connected with all that is important for me. I am a master creator, and I always allow my creation partner to deliver all I choose to me. I stay connected to my creation partner through my powerful and positive thoughts, words, and actions.

I love that I am now making choices that support all that I have intended to experience at my highest level. I love that I am having so much fun now!"

That feels great to me! How about you? If you need to reword the script to make it just right for you, do so. If not, you can use this one. Now affirm and be this person through your thoughts, words, and actions. In fact, know that you already are this person—all you need to do is choose to experience yourself as this person, and you're there.

This life intention becomes the foundation for all of your creations across all areas of your life. When you start any new creation, return to your life intention and make sure the two are aligned.

Your Ideal Health Is Now

Carbs are good for you. Carbs are bad for you. Lifting weights is good for you. Lifting weights is bad for you. Drinking a lot of water is good for you. Drinking a lot of water is bad for you. When it comes to health, the contradictions go on and on. So what are you supposed to do in order to feel and be healthy?

Put your attention on finding a way to feel healthy *that you enjoy!*

When it comes to our health, there seem to be a lot of "have-to's":

- I have to go to the gym.
- I have to give up triple vanilla fudge ice cream.
- I have to run more.
- I have to eat less.
- I have to lose ten pounds.

Of course, these are all "don't wants," but when you feel that everyone else knows more about your health than you do, it's no wonder your health seems to be filled with a bunch of "don't wants." When it comes to our health, we typically defer to the "experts"—but the experts keep changing their minds!

You are the primary expert when it comes to your health and how you feel about it. You can create any exercise or eating program that you want—and you know by now that if it feels good to you, it will be successful!

There are also a lot of erroneous beliefs out there, the most damaging of which is that we have no control over our bodies. Of course, this can't be true, because if we are creators we can't be victims, even when it comes to our health. Again, these principles are absolute, if we think they are. We create in the eternal moment of now, so no matter what our health condition, we can start creating in another direction at any time. We hear stories all the time about how people overcome their illnesses. I hope one day that these stories won't be considered amazing as much as they are commonplace because we have decided to create our health instead of being victims of it.

Health has everything to do with how you *feel* about your health. If you feel like you get sick all the time, you will. If you put your attention on the fact that the flu is going around, you'll probably get it. I live with four children, and people are amazed that I never get the common cold even when I brave the elements in thin sweaters and colds cycle through the family three times! I choose to be healthy, and you can, too!

Start by getting clear on what you really want.

- Do you want to go to the gym, or find a place to exercise that gives you energy?
- Do you want to give up ice cream, or find a way to have a more balanced diet?

- Do you want to run more, or find an exercise that burns calories that is more fun for you?
- Do you want to eat less, or eat more foods that give you energy?
- Do you want to lose ten pounds, or simply look and feel great in your clothes? Or do you want to look and feel fabulous naked?

So set an intention: "I love my healthy and energized body!"

And write your script: "I am so happy and grateful now that I am fit and healthy. I love my exercise routine that fits perfectly into my schedule and is fun and exciting. I love the fact that I found a healthy eating plan that is simple and still delicious. I love all my new energy and that my clothes fit perfectly now. I am so happy that my new healthy lifestyle is so easy to maintain!"

Always start with what you *really* want. If you don't start there, you will shut yourself off from the many possible combinations you could create that you might love.

I really didn't enjoy exercising or limiting the food I loved to eat. Of course, like most people, I tried all sorts of fitness programs that I quickly lost interest in. For years, I listened to all the "experts" and felt they knew all the answers when it came to my health. Later, when that didn't work, I got conscious and started intending to find an exercise and diet program that was easy and natural for me to implement.

There were two things I wanted when it came to exercise:

1. I wanted a quick program of no more than 20 minutes a day.

2. I wanted to use my own body weight, not free weights.

Of course, I also wanted to lose weight. Now, any expert would probably tell you that I wouldn't have that much success with what I wanted. At first glance, what I wanted might seem to be impossible, but I kept my mind open to the possibilities.

Also, there were only two things I wanted when it came to eating:

1. To eat what I wanted.

2. To feel energized by my diet.

So I set my intention, and I just knew that I had already found my program, and that my body looked and felt great!

A couple of weeks later, I read an article that referenced an exercise and eating program derived from an ancient program developed by Tibetan monks. The information intrigued me, so I decided to check it out. I bought a book on the topic and loved the fact that it was used with a person's own body weight, and that the routine took only 15 minutes per day. I knew I was on the right course. The eating program was more about the sequence in which we eat food, not necessarily *what* we eat. This book was giving me exactly what I wanted.

I started the program back in April, and am still doing it every day. The result? I have a ton more energy, and I've lost 25 pounds. So much for difficult, or even impossible, right?

So set your intention on creating a healthy program that you enjoy, and your results will be guaranteed!

Now, what about your general mental health? Can you keep your attention on what you want when your thoughts are filled with fear and anxiety? Of course! Is it easy? Maybe not, but it is worth a try. Raechel did, and this is what happened.

Applying the creation principles got me through the most horrible experience I've ever had in my life. I received *Excuse Me, Your Life Is Waiting* as a gift from my boyfriend's parents upon graduating college in December 2003. I read the book from cover to cover in one sitting. I'd never heard of the Law of Attraction or anything written in the book, but somehow I knew Lynn was on to something. Now, I had a pretty good life as it was, but I still found the book very interesting. I left the book alone for a while and didn't give it much thought.

February of the very next year was the starting point of some very low times for me. My family found out that my mom had cancer in the middle of the month. She went in for two chemotherapy treatments, but she didn't last more than three weeks. My mom passed away on March 8, 2004. On top of that, my boyfriend and I broke up about a month later. This was by far the lowest time in my life. I was a mess, as was the rest of my family. I would lie in my bed for days at a time. I would just stare at the walls or cry. I was so angry and so hurt. I moved to New York to try and get away, but the same behavior continued. I was so depressed, and I couldn't keep a job. This lasted about six months. I would say I was chronically depressed for about a year.

Then I remembered Lynn's book. I read it again. And again. And again. I read it so much that it is now battered and worn. Slowly, I started to feel better. I also started reading other books by authors who wrote about the same things. I eventually got out of my depression and got my life back on track.

I practice the Law of Attraction daily, and my life is as good as it has ever been. I have come to terms with my mom's death, and I can actually find good in it. I can appreciate the time I had with her and the person I am because of her. I still have a lot of work to do, but with my strong foundation and positive outlook,

I'm well on my way. I wish Lynn were here for me to thank. I might not be here if it weren't for her book. I hope this story can inspire others to come from the depths of hell to living a life full of joy and happiness.

Be willing to open your mind to the idea that you are the creator of your health, and use these principles to support you. Then just watch what begins to transpire.

Your Ideal Wealth Is Now

Money is one of the areas of our lives where a lot of us experience the highest degree of difficulty when it comes to creation, and that's because we're missing one very important point: money is a means, a means is a "how," and a "how" is the job of your creation partner.

When you put your attention on the means of creating what you want, you are consciously limiting the power of your creation partner to deliver it for you. Better to give the money a place to flow *to* . . .

I was so happy when I decided what I wanted to do next for work: start my own coaching practice. Once I set my intention, things seemed to fall into place. I started randomly meeting folks who were coaches. I found a training organization that I wanted to attend to get certified. The organization did all their training by phone, so it was very convenient to attend class. The only thing I didn't have was the $3,500 to pay for the training . . .

But I stuck with my intention to be a coach. I didn't water it down to something like, "I intend to earn an extra $3,500 to attend coaching training." When I did slip and think about the "hows," I just couldn't see how it would work. My salary was my salary; it wasn't going to go up all of a sudden. So instead I conjured up the feelings of already being a coach, which meant that the training obviously took care of itself somehow.

One day at work, I got a call from the senior vice president of my division. Now, I didn't work directly for this woman, so I was a little surprised that she was calling me. She said that she wanted to thank me for all the extra work I'd done chairing a committee, and to show her appreciation she was giving me a $7,000 bonus! I had never received a bonus from this company before, or even heard that there were bonuses to be had—and yet here it was!

The point is, you never know how your creation partner is going to orchestrate everything to bring you your heart's desire. I have heard so many people say, as I did, "My salary is my salary." That may be true, but you never know where the means are going to come from. In fact, doesn't it always seem that when we really, really want something, the money shows up?

Another reason it's so important to keep your attention on what you want, as opposed to the money you think you need to make your want happen, is that when you focus on having the money, you are often coming from a place of fear.

Michele wanted to spend more time with her family. In order to do so, she calculated how much it would cost, and she created an investment situation that, when shares vested, would provide her with just enough money to take some time off and be with her family.

This was her ticket, and she knew it. Unfortunately,

it was her only ticket, and if it didn't go through, she wouldn't be able to have the time with her family she craved. She thought about the money a lot; money seemed like the only way to make her wish come true.

Michele chose to put her attention on the business transaction and the attendant fear, instead of her real, primary wish to be with her family and all of the associated good feelings. She was actually choosing to put her attention on something that didn't feel so good. It's no surprise that the transaction failed at the last minute.

Your job is to feel good. Take your attention off the fear of not having the money to do what you want. This will allow your creation partner the freedom to deliver your desires in all kinds of magical ways.

I gave a talk one evening about how to consciously create your experience. At the end of the talk, a woman came up to me and said, "I totally get what you're talking about! I applied it to a trip that I wanted to take around the world!"

Of course, I asked her to tell me more, and she did . . .

I had always wanted to take a trip around the world, but I'd never had the money to actually do it. At one point, my desire started to outweigh my doubt, and I simply decided that I was going to go in March of that year. I certainly didn't have the $30,000 to take the trip, and I had no idea how I was going to get it, but I just knew that I was going on that trip!

I started planning. I researched and decided on a tour company that I wanted to go with, and I even put down the required deposit, which was a lot less than $30,000. Some people thought I was crazy to put down a deposit without having the remaining money, but I just knew that the rest would come, so I just kept planning!

A couple of months before I was set to go, I got a letter from a lawyer who said that I was going to be inheriting some money. The amount was said to be around $10,000. I thought that would be a big help, so I was very excited!

My departure date was fast approaching, and I kept right on planning and even started buying the clothes and luggage I would need for the trip. I simply never doubted that the money would be there.

About two weeks before I was to leave, the inheritance settlement came in. It wasn't for $10,000—it was for $30,000!

Now there are plenty of people out there who have used these principles to create wealth. In the movie, *The Secret* (www.thesecret.tv), Jack Canfield, co-founder of the bestselling Chicken Soup for the Soul series, talks about how he used the Law of Attraction to create $100,000 one year. That was his intention, and he got it. Now, of course, he earns millions upon millions. The important thing was that he started somewhere!

All of us have the ability to create any amount of money in our experience, but most of us run into a small glitch when we say we want "money." Our beliefs about money run the gamut:

- Money is scarce.
- I don't deserve money.
- Money is evil.
- I can't handle a lot of money.

I had a conversation the other day with someone about money. He said he wanted more of it, so I asked him what was the first word that came to his mind when I said the word "money." His response? "Lack."

A lot of people have created a relationship with money based on mistrust. We don't trust that it is available to us, that it will come back when we spend it, and that it is always there when we need it.

The word "money" even makes us feel badly!

So if your intention is to make $100,000 in one year, and you think and feel lack when you say the word "money," do you think you'll attract $100,000? Nope!

So how do you change your relationship with money? Create a new one, of course!

"Don't wants":

- I don't want to go bankrupt.
- I don't want to lose money.
- I don't want to be in debt.
- I don't want to be a slave to money.
- I don't want to feel lack.

"Do wants":

- I want to have plenty of money.
- I want to pay for things in cash.
- I want to earn some of my money doing work I love.
- I want money to come into my experience effortlessly.
- I want financial freedom.

Set your intention: "Money pours into my experience easily and effortlessly now!"

And your script: "I am so happy and grateful now that I know that money is one of the many means to experience all that I want. I love the fact that money comes from unexpected sources and flows into my life as much as I allow it to flow out. I love that I trust that my financial picture is one filled with abundance. I am grateful that I have the freedom to experience any experience I choose."

If you are not comfortable with the word "money," then change it to a word you might be more comfortable with, like "abundance," "finance," or "prosperity." Again, your script has to feel great and be believable! Now be the person who has money today. Think, speak, and act like it.

One of my intentions is to attract at least $15,000 a month. Notice how I didn't limit it to "earning $15,000 a month." The words are important. In order to be the person who attracts at least $15,000 a month, I choose to think thoughts of abundance and prosperity. Instead of complaining about gas prices, I say thank you every time I fill up my tank. In my world, my business thrives no matter what the economy is doing. I don't walk out of a store and whine: "I can't believe someone would spend that much on a T-shirt." Because I have at least $15,000, I *can* believe.

Now, acting is the fun part. How do you act like the person who attracts at least $15,000 a month, when you don't actually have $15,000? Simple, you spend money when it feels right. You don't deny yourself that second cup of coffee. Why would you? You have at least $15,000. You turn on the air conditioner and don't worry about the bill. Why would you? You have at least $15,000.

I think you get my point. Remember, take the action that feels good to you. Going out and buying a Mercedes when you are in debt doesn't feel good, so don't do it. Going out to dinner when you haven't splurged in a long time might feel good. So start there.

Financial freedom is not about having truckloads of money; it's in knowing that your relationship with money is one that you trust, and that money will be there when you want it. It means you know money is important, but it's only one of the means to having all that you want. It's about trusting that your creation partner will always deliver what you choose for yourself without fail! Now, that's financial freedom! In essence, when you are free from needing money, you have the power to choose to have it in your experience.

Now for a little fun . . .

If you believe the Creation Foundation Belief that *my creation partner delivers for me what I choose without fail,* why not choose to get a tenfold return on every penny you spend? Talk about creating a great relationship with money—you actually believe it's going to come back to you when you spend it!

What do I mean? Well, when you buy your $3 cup of coffee, thank the universe for your $30 return. When you fill up at the gas station, say thank you to the universe for your $300 return. When you pay $100 for your electric bill, say thanks for the $1,000 return. Why not? It's fun, it keeps your attention on what you want, and it doesn't take much time. It also keeps your positive energy flowing when you are spending money, thus keeping you connected to the source that is going to bring more money into your experience.

I have been doing this for a while, and I have never felt more in control of my financial situation! This is what freedom is all about.

Your Ideal Romance Is Now

As you know, during the writing of this book, my relationship of seven years ended. I should explain that this was more than just a relationship, as my partner and I shared a home and have a child; we were a family. We shared all the responsibilities of a married couple, just without the actual license.

I've already said that life got really hard for us financially, and there was a lot of doubt about what we were going to do. During this time, we both allowed our fears to bring out the worst in us, and so the relationship ended.

Reading this, you may wonder what I have wondered: if I am the creator of my experience, why would I create such a heartbreaking event? The answer was tough to swallow at first, but it became very clear, after the anger, outrage, and sorrow had passed, that I actually created what I ultimately wanted—my freedom! Even though I did the one thing I have asked you not to do—I started creating with an intention that wasn't truly authentic—I still got what I wanted in the end.

When I started my relationship, I thought I knew who I was and what I wanted. I lived in a great one-bedroom apartment. My life was simple, and I liked it that way. My partner moved in soon after we started dating, and I loved our time together there. Then all the "shoulds" started popping up. We should buy a house; we should have a child; we should do this and that.

If I had spoken my truth at the time, I would have said that I loved the life we already had and that I didn't want all the "shoulds." But what did I do instead? I did what I always had done: I did what I thought I should do. I did the responsible thing. I did the exact opposite of what I really wanted. I even scripted the white picket fence!

This is not at all easy to admit. I stand by all of my choices, and I regret nothing. I have loved the entire experience, and I wouldn't trade it for the world. But that doesn't mean that now that I know my real truth, I can't act on it and be free to create in a direction that I think will help me to experience even more happiness!

When it comes to ideal partners, so much of our attention is on "the other"—who they are, what they do, what they want, what their interests are, how cute their hair looks all disheveled in the morning, etc. But now it's time to take a different strategy, and shift that spotlight so it's shining right on you.

Would I date me?

Good question. Would you? Remember, attraction is attraction. If you want to attract your ideal partner, then you have to *become* your ideal partner!

So would you date you?

Shift your intention to creating the ideal relationship with yourself first.

"Don't wants":

• I don't want to be controlling with myself.
• I don't want to second-guess myself.
• I don't want to spend time doing things I don't want to do.
• I don't want to sacrifice my desires.
• I don't want to lose myself.

"Do wants":

• I want to be free.
• I want to be clear on who I am and what I want.
• I want to speak my truth with myself and others at all times.
• I want to be an individual.
• I want to do things that bring me joy.
• I want to experience my life as my own, and every other relationship as a bonus.

Your powerful positive intention: "I choose to be authentically me, so that I naturally attract my ideal partnership!"

And your script: "I am so happy and grateful now that I am authentically who I am at all times; that I share who I am with everyone I am in relation with; that I think, speak, and act my truth at all times; that my life is filled with the experiences that I have chosen; that I now trust myself to follow my inner voice, without fail; that I now know that I have everything I want within me and can enjoy my experiences for what they really are—simply experiences I have chosen to create. I love, trust, accept all that I am and now choose to share myself with my ideal partner."

In fact, if you could become that person, even *I* would date you. I mean, theoretically, of course!

When you become the person you want to date, not only will you attract the partner of your dreams, you will also attract all sorts of people who are compatible with you!

Your Ideal Work Is Now

Did you know that every time you walk into a room full of people, at least half of them are dissatisfied with their work? That's right, 56 percent of the U.S. population is feeling pretty grumbly about their jobs.

So why is it? It's simple: people are dissatisfied with their work because they are doing work they think they should be doing or have to do, instead of work they want to do.

What are you doing?

Have you created your work experience unconsciously?

One thing I invite you to do right now is stop seeking your life purpose. Trust me, I spent a long time doing just that in corporations I didn't like because I thought I couldn't make a move without knowing what I was supposed to be doing. Then I realized that all I needed to know was what I wanted to do next and start creating that. Think about it: what word feels better— "seeking" or "creating"?

So how do you consciously create your work? Well,

at the risk of sounding like a broken record, it's always the same process. First, ask yourself, *What* don't *I want anymore?* This will probably be simple, so let's dig in! List all the things you don't want in your next job. Maybe you're tired of . . .

• Your grouchy boss.
• Those two measly weeks of vacation.
• The chain holding you to your desk.
• Feeling undervalued.
• Feeling underfunded.
• The long, smoggy commute.
• Those slow-motion Mondays.
• The time away from your family.
• The work that doesn't challenge your brain.
• Those co-workers who are more of a pain than a help.
• That glacial air-conditioning under that bleak neon sun.

And that's just a start . . . The more thorough you are with your "don't wants," the more you will be able to come up with some fantastic "do wants," so take your time with this. Get it all out!

When you get all those "don't wants" off your chest, it's time to start turning the tide. So what is your negative truth about your job? Is it that you . . .

• Hate your job?
• Have to settle for a job you don't love in order to pay the bills?
• Think the job you would love doesn't exist?
• Think you are not qualified to do work you love?

Which one describes your situation most accurately? Find the one that really hits home for you, the one that holds you back the most from having satisfying work.

Now, take your negative truth and make it your new positive truth.

"I will never find work I love that generates the income I really want" becomes "I am doing work I love, and I am making more than the income I always thought I wanted."

Without your new powerful positive intention, you will remain stuck in your old negative truth, and you will not be able to see the possibilities of what you can create. Recite your new truth every day, and during every moment when you start to have negative thoughts about what you want next. Make it your new mantra!

Now it's time to bless your current circumstance because it's your very dissatisfaction that's prodding you to your next level of career happiness. Remember, you can't create in a positive direction if you are coming from a negative reaction. So it's time to find positive things you can focus on in your current job to be grateful for.

Here are some ideas . . .

• Your short commute.
• The money you are making.
• Your benefits.
• Some fulfilling daily activities.
• Some fun co-workers.
• Working in a great building.
• The fact that you have a job.

Answer this question: *what does my job allow me to be, do, or have that not having it wouldn't?* Then put your attention on being grateful for all of those things. When negative thoughts about your job start to creep in, take your attention off your negative truth and put it on your positive one.

The goal is to change your overall attitude so that

you can open your mind to the possibility of what you can create next.

Next—you know the drill—take your list of "don't wants" and turn them into your new "do wants." This is where we get to leave the miserable ballast behind and start creating! Get centered on your positive truth and start writing your "What I Want to Have Next" list. In other words, dream! Here are some ideas . . .

- A boss I can partner with and learn from.
- At least four weeks of vacation.
- A job where I am in and out of the office.
- A company where I feel completely valued financially and personally.
- Making exactly the salary I want.
- A short and enjoyable commute.
- A great day every day.
- Plenty of time with my family.
- Work that challenges and inspires me.
- Great co-workers who partner in getting results.
- Telecommuting.

What did you come up with? As always, be sure that your "do wants" are very positive and not just "don't wants" in disguise. The rule is that they have to inspire you! Saying them out loud should leave you feeling pretty darn good.

When you are tempted to say, "Yeah, but . . . ," stop yourself and speak your new positive truth. This process is all about changing how you think and feel so that you can change your circumstances to what you want.

Now the fun part . . . Design your ideal job description. How does the phrase "job search" hit you? It just makes me cringe. In fact, the process of a job search strikes fear in the minds of many highly qualified and capable persons. Why? For many reasons, but the main one is that most job searches start with the belief that you have no control over the process. You are a "victim" of the job market, a pawn at the mercy of human resources departments and resume reviewers. You have no control over the process or, ultimately, what job you get in the end. So how do you become the creator of your job? Use the principles! Start by designing your ideal job description. This is less about *where* you want to work and more about *how* you want to work.

Jane was frustrated. She had left her previous job and now wanted enjoyable work. She was spending her time looking at employment ads, trying to fit herself and her skills into what she was seeing.

Jane had never heard, much less ever thought, that she had the opportunity to write her ideal job description. Her experience had always been like most people's experience: you search for a job, not create one.

Jane was willing to give it a stab. She started with a wish list that sounded like a big old list of don't wants:

- I don't want a long commute.
- I don't want to work long hours.
- I don't want to have to bring my work home with me.
- I don't want to lose my vacation time.
- I don't want to do boring work with boring people.
- I need health insurance.

After we talked, she started to understand that the process of scripting is really about creating a picture in which you already have what you want.

Jane got the message and started getting serious about what this ideal job description was going to be for her.

"I am so happy now that I have found the job of my dreams. I love the fact that my office is a ten-minute commute and that it is even in opposite traffic! I love the people I work with. They are creative and fun to be around. Everyone gets along well, and my boss is more like a partner than a boss. I love that I am now using all of my writing, editing, and PR skills in my position, and that my work is appreciated and valued. I love that this is project work and that I can see it through start to finish. I enjoy my four weeks of vacation and love that my medical is paid in full! I am so fulfilled now that I am finally doing work I love."

Jane then decided to let up on searching the job listings and just put her attention on her script. Two weeks later, Jane was inspired once again to check out the job listings and came upon a description that matched her script!

Do you think Jane would have been attracted to that description had she not been putting her attention on her script? No way! She would have blown right by it because she didn't know what she wanted; she was too busy searching for what she "thought" she "could" have.

And if working for someone else is just not your cup of tea anymore, then . . .

Your Ideal Business Is Now

If you have made the amazing choice to follow your dreams by creating a business you love that allows you some glorious freedom, please, please, please don't settle for less than you have envisioned.

I started my own coaching practice because I simply did not fit into a corporate environment, even after trying to blend for 15 years. I felt the work I was doing in my gray cubicle was not, in the grand scheme of things, all that important. Also, I craved freedom—freedom to do the work I loved, in the way I wanted to do it!

When we decide to start something new, like a business, what do we typically do? Often, one of the first things we do, even before we decide what kind of business we want, is go to the "experts." What do they say?

- Starting a business is hard.
- You always have to manage the risk.
- It is hard to get start-up money.
- Most businesses fail in the first five years.
- Being an entrepreneur takes all your time.
- Owning your own business is a huge commitment.
- You will have to do a lot of things you don't like.
- You really won't start turning a profit for the first several years.

Wow, you haven't even started, and you're already filled with fear, doubt, and worry! What kind of entrepreneurial experience do you think you are creating for yourself by listening to these naysayers? Unless you're hoping to create a company of broken hearts, a café of dead-end dreams, or a soundtrack to gloom, perhaps you should consult yourself instead.

Why are there plenty of successful entrepreneurs out there? You guessed it: they created their businesses the way they wanted to!

And hey, who's to say—other than you, that is—that you can't create a business that brings you a ton of financial opportunity without trading all of your time and the things that are important to you? The Law of Attraction is the same whether you are creating a multinational business or a tasty afternoon snack: what you put your thoughts and feelings on, you create.

So don't listen to the experts—at least not unless you're sure about what you want to create, and you only need some friendly help during the process. You are the expert in your life. Trust yourself. The time to seek out experts is when you are clear on what you have chosen to create. Remember, let your creation partner bring the right experts to you. In other words, don't ask an expert what kind of business to start or how to market yourself or how to rate your ideas or to quell your bubbling enthusiasm with some hard, cold facts. Instead, decide what business you want to run, what marketing activities you enjoy, and how you want to fire it up.

As I mentioned earlier, various experts said that I wouldn't get clients to pay my coaching fees if I didn't do a bunch of marketing activities that I really didn't enjoy. I listened for a while, tried to implement them, and surprise, surprise, they didn't work. Or they worked like a drippy faucet when I wanted a waterfall. The funny thing was, I actually had more clients before I started listening to the experts! I was focused on someone else's "shoulds," "don'ts," and "have-tos," so I wasn't getting my desired results.

It took me some time to realize that I wasn't feeling good doing all of the tasks. When I understood that I was attracting mediocre results because I was feeling mediocre about what I was doing, I changed my tack.

I knew that I enjoyed writing and speaking, so I started doing them more. I created coaching programs that I felt would deliver great value to my clients, and I didn't do research on pricing; I just priced them at what I thought was fair. I decided that my ideal clients were going to come to me primarily through word-of-mouth or through my writing or speaking. I finally stopped doing everything the experts said! And then magical things started happening:

• As you know, I got a book deal, and how could I top that?

- I wrote a little pro bono article that was filed away on the directory of a major self-help Web site. One evening, I started getting a ton of e-mails from people registering for my e-mail list. I had no idea where these folks were coming from. I found out later that my article had been included in the newsletter sent out by the self-help site. I have no idea how the article got in the newsletter; I guess my creation partner was supporting me! As a side note, that newsletter went out to over a hundred thousand people!

I had been in touch with the founder of www.journey-to-success.com to ask her how she set up her Web site. I thought it might be nice to work with her someday. A couple of months later, I felt inspired to jump on her site, and I noticed that she had posted several teleseminars hosted by people not affiliated with her site. I thought that she might be interested in me doing one, so I shot her an e-mail. She wrote back that at the moment she received my e-mail, she'd been sitting there wondering who she was going to get on such short notice to host her July teleseminar! Needless to say, I got the job.

Putting my attention on what I wanted and only doing those things that I really enjoyed worked! Not only that, my main source of new clients is from word-of-mouth referrals!

Rebecca, owner of a freelance musician-booking company, really started to believe that she could attract her ideal clients.

I had lots of clients coming in, but hated doing all the follow-up e-mails and calls I believed were required to get each client to book my services. What I really wanted was for prospective customers to contact me, talk to me, listen to the demo CD I provided, and then book a music ensemble soon after. I did NOT want to "waste" my time "chasing" each person who inquired about my services. In addition, I wanted to make more money per job and to spread out the jobs each month so that they wouldn't all end up on the same day and time.

A few weeks after putting my intention out for this kind of a customer, I noticed that people were booking soon after speaking to me. I also raised my rates, had an easy time saying no to the gigs that conflicted with ones I'd already booked (instead of piling on a bunch of commitments all at the same time), worked out a very easy process for clients to hear my demo CD online, and discovered an easy way to write contracts. Oh, yeah, I also wanted to have clients whom I enjoyed working with, and who were good at communication. Did I get that, too? You bet I did!

The customers continue to roll in easily now, and I feel so relaxed about the way they come to me.

Rebecca stopped believing what everyone was telling her about what she should do to market her business, and she put her attention on what she wanted to do. Her business is thriving because of it.

Rebecca and I both consciously changed our relationship with our businesses. Before we did this, we weren't experiencing freedom. In fact, at times I felt more smothered by my own business than I'd ever felt in corporate America! Rebecca and I went from feeling obligated to our businesses to allowing ourselves and our businesses to grow naturally. When we stopped forcing, we could really love and enjoy our work more, and the clients started pouring in.

So, what kind of relationship do you have with your

business or the business you dream of building? Spend some time answering the following questions:

- What is my ideal business?
- What is my ideal job description?
- Who is my ideal client?
- What do I enjoy doing that would attract my ideal clients?
- What kind of relationship do I want to have with my business?

Whether you are thinking of starting a business, or you already run a business that you are not 100 percent satisfied with, the manifestation process is the same.

"Don't wants":

- To fail.
- To be consumed by my business.
- To go broke.
- To have to sell or market my services.

"Do wants":

- To run a successful business.
- To have time for all the things I enjoy in life.
- To have money pour in.
- To have clients pour in.

Why not? You're the creator of this business. Why can't it be just as you choose for it to be? It's simple—if you don't believe that you can own a business and actually have more time off than when you worked for someone else, you can't. If you don't believe your creation partner will deliver you the ideas, people, circumstances, and events that will support your choice, it won't. If you don't believe you can work from your house just as efficiently and successfully as you could from an office, you can't. If you don't believe you can come up with the money to launch your incredible idea, you can't. Your creation partner can only create through you what *you* have chosen.

So what do you want? Now, your powerful positive intention: "I am now earning money doing work I love!"

What is yours? Maybe it's: "I am now running a business delivering services that I feel are important while generating the revenue I choose."

Now ask yourself:

• Is this what I really want?
• How does my intention make me feel?
• Is it in alignment with my life intention?

If your intention makes you feel powerful and positive, then you are ready to move on to your script. And remember to be the person who thinks, speaks, and acts like the person who has a great relationship with your business.

Now write your script: "I am so happy and grateful now that I have a thriving business. I love that I am only doing the tasks that I enjoy and that I have found ways to offload those I didn't enjoy. I love how my ideal clients seem to flow into my experience easily and effortlessly. I am happy that I have created this business so that I have plenty of time with my family. I love how it feels so natural for me to run my business and that I have plenty of time to enjoy its success."

Robert works in finance. Recently, he mustered some courage to do what he wanted—and it worked.

When I was a mortgage broker, I was also selling a debt-reduction program for $1,000 and a wealth-creation seminar for $7,500. Those two products netted me $7,000 each time I sold a set. But I wasn't selling a lot, and clients were just trickling in. What I recognized was that I really enjoyed selling the debt-reduction program, but I didn't enjoy selling the wealth-creation seminar.

At times, I still can't believe I had the courage to make this choice, but I decided that because I didn't feel good about selling the wealth-creation seminar, I should just stop. So I did. I willingly cut my potential income by thousands of dollars! You would be surprised at how good it felt to drop something that I just didn't feel good about.

Within a few months, my sales tripled! After that, I was approached by a company to sell their debt-management program—which I loved—for five to ten times more than I was making! Now I earn more money per month than I used to make in three!

So there you have it, the heavy hitters—health, wealth, romance, and work. All are equal in the eyes of the creation principles. Now you just have to believe that they are equal in your beliefs about them. So go ahead and create your new powerful, positive relationships in these areas. Doing so will guarantee your success in creating what you want in each!

Creation Principles Really Work!

"I had just gotten my 16-month-old twins out of the tub. I was in the hallway chasing one baby and trying to get a diaper on her while the other one was playing with toys on the bathroom floor. As I was chasing her, I had the thought, *Wow, I'm so lucky. I've never had a problem with them pooping in the tub during a bath or having one poop on the floor while I'm getting the other one diapered.* (Let me tell you, it is a challenge to chase both around and successfully get diapers on both!) Then I noticed that my attention and feelings shifted to, *What a mess that would be to clean up!* I bet you can guess what happened next . . . about two minutes later, I had the diaper on the first baby and went to retrieve the second one. She had a line of eight poop balls in a trail on the floor behind her!"

—Sherri

SIX

Excuse Me, but . . . I Still Have a Lot of Questions about This Creation Business!

> The reality is we have come here to thrive, and prosper and live this grand human experience in lighthearted joy, not in struggle and pain.
>
> —Lynn Grabhorn,
> *Excuse Me, Your Life Is Waiting*

Over time, I have gotten a lot of questions from my clients who are in the process of getting conscious and using the creation principles. Both the questions and answers are invaluable, so I thought I would include them for you here. Pay special attention, as they are questions you will probably have as you begin your own creation journey.

What If I Really Don't Know What I Want?

If you don't feel that it is okay to *want*, then you will continue to create unconsciously. If you say things like, "I should just be happy with what I have," or "Isn't it selfish to want more?" or even "I don't deserve more," then you will have a lot of trouble knowing what you want because you are unconsciously creating more not wanting.

Try to think of something that has stayed the same—never changed. Can you come up with anything? It's pretty tough, isn't it? Then why would you expect that *you* won't change—change what you think, who you are, what you want? We are all evolving, and evolving means change. So why not choose the change that we really want? It is our nature to experience more, so you have every right to want more. In fact, it is your birthright!

Depending on the area of your life and the degree of creation difficulty you've assigned to it, you may sometimes feel like you just don't know what you want. So here's a handy tool to get out of those confusion blues: while what you ultimately want may be blurred, you still know what you want right now—you want to know what you want next! So create your knowing!

First, let's start with the statement, "I don't know what I want next"—a big "don't want." By now you know exactly what you are attracting—more "don't wants." So the first step is to flip it. Make the statement, "I am so happy and grateful now that I know exactly what I want next." Feel better? Then you're moving in the right direction.

How many times have you asked yourself a question and not answered it? Here's an example, "Why does this always happen to me?" or "How could I let that happen?" or "Why don't I know what I want next?" We ask, but we don't wait for our answer. The answer is always there, hovering around inside you, waiting for you to be aware of it.

When you ask yourself, "What do I want next?" and you don't wait for the answer, it's probably because you already know the answer—and it scares you. Maybe it feels like a boogey-man. And it's probably followed by a big fat "but"!

If I had asked myself what I really wanted—to stay in my apartment or to buy a house—I would have said to stay in my apartment. What did I say to myself instead? I said, "I would love to stay in my apartment with my partner, but what if that's not what she wants and she decides to move on without me?" Then I followed it with all the justifications . . . it's crazy to throw away money on rent, a house would give us so much more room, maybe this is the next step in our relationship. On and on I went until I talked myself into it and thought it was exactly what I wanted to do next.

How many times have you talked yourself *out* of knowing what you want next like I did? A lot of us simply don't know that we know, and so we choose to talk ourselves out of it. Trust me, if you have to write up a list of pros and cons, you are talking yourself out of what you really want!

So how do you rip up that list and really know, in your gut, what you want? It all comes down to how you feel. Set the intention that you will *feel* your answer, and ask yourself the important questions. In my case, my options were to stay in my apartment or buy a house. If I had been honest about which one felt better, I would have chosen to stay in my apartment—and that would have felt great!

Ask yourself how *you* feel about A or B. If you have more than two options, question how you feel about each of them. Choose the one that feels better, and then go through the same process until you come up with the one that feels best.

I can't tell you the number of times I have posed this question to clients, and the answer instantly becomes crystal-clear to them. When we start the conversation, I can hear the confusion in their voices. As soon as they choose the idea that feels better, their voices become very clear and calm. They already know their answer!

The question, "What do I want?" then becomes, "How do I overcome my fear and *choose* what I really want?"

Remember when I talked about flipping the process of being from thinking, speaking, and then acting, to acting, speaking, and then thinking? That's what you want to do here. You want to circumvent your tortured thoughts, your list of "buts," your flimsy pros and cons, your sensible "shoulds," and act like the person who has already spoken your truth about what you really want. You want to speak your truth! Only after speaking your truth to yourself first, admitting what you really want and knowing that it is perfectly okay to want it, can you speak your truth to others.

In my housing situation, my first step should have been to stop myself at my "but" and just know that it felt right for me to stay in my apartment. Once I was honest about (and accepting of) my choice, I could have talked with my partner, knowing that what I wanted was fine and what she would choose to do would be fine as well. I know this sounds hard, but looking back, it would have been a cakewalk compared to having the conversation about ending our relationship because we were both so unhappy with the series of dishonest choices we had made. Truth is more easily front-loaded, but it always comes out in the end.

Knowing what you really want is all about listening to how you feel and trusting that what you feel will always be the indication of your best direction. How could it not? The Law of Attraction means like attracts like (remember?), so feel-good feelings will always attract more feel-good feelings. In the end, isn't that what we really want next?

How Do I Feel Rich When I Don't Have Any Money?

I think it's so important to reiterate the fact that the creation principles work. No . . . matter . . . what. Like attracts like, so a feeling of having no money attracts more not having any. This may be the biggest hurdle you have to overcome, especially when the bills are piling up, the creditors are calling, and the mortgage payment is coming due.

Not having money and having the responsibility of providing for your family can be the most frightening experience of your life—no question! It was in Robert's case.

It had been almost four years since I got laid off from a dot.com company. I had been struggling to work on my own since then. I tried a half-dozen businesses; some made some money, but not consistently, and never enough to pay the bills. My partner was not happy because she felt I wasn't pulling my weight. I never really worried much about money, but at that point I was beginning to feel the pressure. Bills were just piling up. At one point, I called my friend Tony and cried because we were on the cusp of declaring bankruptcy. I could hardly believe the words were coming out of my mouth.

The past few years were all about struggling to find a way to get ahead or at least break even. The 25 years before that I was always making six figures plus, but was always working paycheck to paycheck.

As I mentioned before, I was in the same predicament as Robert. How badly I felt about myself was in direct proportion to the height of the bills piling up. I didn't even want to go to the mailbox anymore! I hated myself during this time, actually *hated* myself. I was personalizing my circumstance, thereby creating more and more bills!

I remember sitting in my room, panicked about how I was ever going to get my mortgage out of foreclosure—when it hit me like a ton of bricks. For the past two years, I had chosen to unconsciously experience financial struggle. I chose it! Me! And you know what? I was doing a great job at manifesting that experience! I accepted in that moment that I had created my circumstances, and when I did, it freed me to make a new choice. So I chose to experience vast financial wealth. I can't describe the sense of calm that came over me, but it felt something like sitting by a clear mountain lake in the early morning. I realized that the key to getting my mortgage out of foreclosure wasn't money; it was for me to consciously choose to get my mortgage in the green again.

By accepting my circumstance and knowing it had nothing to do with who I was—only what I was choosing to experience—I regained my power to create in a new direction. I finally understood the Creation Foundation Belief that *I am not my current circumstance; I am the creator of it!*

I could start feeling good again. And that, in turn, allowed me to find solutions to my immediate problems and set up my intentions for my whole financial picture. Robert had a similar experience with similar results.

I had always been a pretty upbeat, happy person, but never understood that I was the one in control of my happiness, not circumstances. I started watching my thoughts and the feelings they were creating in me. Once I started doing that, I felt better. I was able to start making choices to increase my income in ways that I had never done before, ways that I felt good about! Changing how I felt about my circumstances and putting my attention on what I really wanted are what changed my financial tide!

Choosing my thoughts—the ones that make me feel good—and then taking action has created even more financial opportunities way beyond what I ever used to dream possible. Not only will all of my debts (almost a million dollars) be paid in just 2.6 years (down from 30 years!), but my bank accounts are growing, I can pay cash for everything I want, I take more vacations, and I give more money away. I have something now that money only provides for in a small way: I know that I can have money and things, but most important, I feel really good about what I do every day.

No matter what you are unhappy with, at some point you will realize that having your attention on the problem is only attracting more problem. And you'll realize that having your attention on being incapable will attract more incapable. Focusing your attention on your circumstances, rather than on who you are, will attract more of the exact same circumstances.

Remember, you are not your circumstances; you are the person experiencing your circumstances. And they are as temporary as you allow them to be. The sooner you get your attention on what you really want and not on the fact that it's not here yet, the sooner you will create your new desired experience.

It is the same when it comes to money. Money flows

according to how you feel about it. If you feel that it doesn't flow into your experience, then it won't. I decided that money flows effortlessly into my experience—and now it does. It can for you, too!

How Do I Get Others on Board?

When you start implementing creation principles, you may meet with resistance from family and friends. This can make it hard to stay focused on your wants, but it can be made easier when you accept that you *can't* get everyone else on board. No matter why you want to get them on board, you just can't—and you really don't need to. Once you accept this, you can get your attention back on creating your experience, which is the only way you can influence those around you anyway.

All you need to do is consciously choose to demonstrate these principles in your own life, day in and day out. Without expecting to convert anyone else, demonstrate your truth.

A lot of folks want to get others on board for a lot of different reasons. Some want to help others to create their own experience. Some want to feel understood and supported in their own creations. Whatever the reason, if you have your attention on someone else's experience, you don't have it on your own. When you put your attention on what someone else is "not" doing, you don't have your attention on what you have chosen to create. In fact, you have put your attention on something you don't want.

Wanting someone else on board also implies a hidden need. It might go something like this: "If so and so isn't on board, then I can't create what I want." This is just not true! You already have all your need inside of you; you don't need someone else to agree, approve, or even do anything in order to have what you want. On top of that, your creation partner takes care of the "how." You may think you need someone else, but it's not your job to know who or how. Your job is to know and stay focused on the "what."

My client, Mark, once asked me, "How do I keep my creation vibration up when my people around me don't believe these principles, and they push my buttons?" I replied to Mark with a simple question, "Why do you have buttons in the first place?"

The important thing to focus on is not what others are doing or not doing to us, but what they are helping us to reveal about ourselves. That is why they don't have to be on board with these principles at all. What Mark did was create a situation where, through the actions of others, he recognized that he had "buttons" that could be pushed. Now he can consciously choose to eliminate those buttons so that he can continue to stay connected and create by keeping his attention on what he really wants.

Consciously keeping your attention on what you are thinking, saying, and doing—and not on what others are thinking, saying, and doing—brings the experiences you have chosen into your reality. When that happens, others around you will naturally be curious and may want to know what you are doing and why your life seems to be so great. They may reject what you are doing, but that is really not your concern; you know that allowing another's experience to change your positive flow will hinder your creation progress. More important than getting someone else on board is keeping your attention on what you want—consistent results with these principles.

Living your truth is the best way to help others anyway. Nan has a story about doing just that.

Iwas raised in South Dakota with all the typical "shoulds" and "shouldn'ts." I remember being very concerned about what others thought, and the Golden Rule was not to let anyone know what was going on within the walls of our house. Appearances were very important, and divorce had a definite stigma. Although I was intelligent and well-liked in school, I found myself sabotaging relationships with men because of internal turmoil.

This was back in the '70s, and the majority of my peers were married before they got out of college. I was one of the last of my friends to wed; I had nightmares that others thought there was something wrong with me. I (finally) got married in my mid-twenties. I met my husband at work, and I slipped into the relationship comfortably. "Comfortably" meant that our turbulent relationship was familiar to me. He was an alcoholic. Alcoholism was my family's dysfunction. I understand now that that was what we were hiding when I was younger. Needless to say, the marriage did not match my fairy-tale vision. I was unhappy, but because of my upbringing, the thought of divorce was out of the question. After eight years, I knew I had to do something, but the fear was too great. My self-esteem was at an all-time low. A year later, after going to Al-Anon and several therapists, I decided to get a divorce.

I remember the day I approached my dad to let him know what I planned to do. But, lo and behold, instead of being disappointed in me, he was supportive. I didn't have to tell him I was unhappy; he had seen it for years. My own fear had kept me in prison.

Looking back, my ex's behavior under the influence turned out to be the greatest gift. With his assistance, I hit my rock bottom and surrendered to my Higher Power, which supported me to make changes and move on with my life. We had both slipped into a relationship that was a familiar reflection of the dysfunction we had both been raised with.

The day I decided to file for divorce, I not only set myself free, I set my whole family free as well. Just three months later, my brother Jim called and said, "Thank you. I am getting a divorce, too." My righteous older brother, Don, who condemned my divorce at the time, got a divorce a year later. Three years after that, my mom moved to North Carolina on her own. I think my mom had visions of my dad following her to her dream place. Instead, my dad retired in the Colorado mountains. Mind you, my folks never got divorced, but they never lived together again either. Twenty years later, my baby brother, Mike, got a divorce.

I'd had no idea that the choice I made for myself would affect others. Perhaps it was a coincidence, perhaps not. I just knew I had to do something, or I was going to die inside. The good news is that we all created better lives for ourselves with the decisions we made.

On another happy note, 15 years later, after both my ex and I had received support from various sources, we came back into each other's lives, and we are now best friends. We both took personal responsibility for the divorce—he for his behavior while under the influence, and me for being the "great enabler."

After my divorce, however, I was still attracted to alcoholics. After a few years of inner work, I started attracting recovering alcoholics. Now, after many years of inner work, my relationships are alcoholic-free. I knew I had to change myself in order to attract what I wanted in my life. I'm still fine-tuning, and my life just keeps on getting better.

Nan wasn't consciously trying to help her family members end relationships she thought were bad for them. She put her attention on being honest about her own relationship and doing what it took, even though she didn't feel accepted. By changing her life, she demonstrated to her family that it was okay to change in order to be happy, thus freeing them to do the same for themselves.

These principles prove over and over again that the more we put attention on applying them to ourselves, the more those around us benefit. Sometimes it seems easier to try to save other people because we think we know what they really need. In truth, we can't possibly know what they need; they are, like us, still trying to figure out who they really are and what they really want for themselves. Paying attention to ourselves and being honest at all costs, not evangelizing, is how we help others to do the same. As Gandhi said, "Be the change you want to see in the world."

When you feel that you are moving your attention from yourself and putting it on another person's problems, know that you are distracting yourself from your own work. Ask yourself, "What am I not changing in myself right now that needs changing?" and "Why am I avoiding making this change?"

Focusing on others always turns out to be a distraction; paying attention and understanding why you are choosing to distract yourself will help you to get reimmersed in your own creation story.

Can We Teach Creation Principles to Our Children?

Do you sometimes feel that you wouldn't be so "messed up" today if only your parents had taught you about creation principles when you were young? Sadly, few people consciously implement these principles in their lives, and thus most people don't have the tools to teach them to their children. But you can be one of the people who turns the tide with your family. Wouldn't it feel good knowing you could show your children how to create everything they want in life? So, how can you teach your children about these principles?

In Lynn's book, she told about a little slugger named Jessie. He was a little baseball player with a big swing. When Lynn asked him how he hit so many home runs, his reply was, "I dunno. Each time I get up to bat, I just feel what it's going to be like to connect, and I do."

Kids naturally know this stuff if we allow them to! All we need to do is reinforce it. I have learned to let my daughter Sammi be and experience what she wants, and how she wants it, as long as she's not in any danger. Of course, this does take some practice. When she asked me for a cup of milk mixed with lemon soda water and regular water, my first thought was "Yuck!" But my second thought was, "How do I know? I never tried it!" In the end, it didn't matter what I thought; she loved her citrus milky substance to the hilt!

The greatest gift we can give to our children, and to anyone for that matter, is to allow them to have their own experience. No one, not even a child, needs our judgment or disapproval.

So allow and share, but don't preach! When Robert wants his teenage daughter to watch something he thinks is interesting, he doesn't tell her to watch it. He watches it when she is around, and she usually comes, sits down, and asks what it's about. Now that's allowing!

And, most important, *be* with your children.

My daughter Tee is 11, and we recently listened to Lynn's CD series together in the car. We listened to the first CD on the way to her gymnastics practice. Tee has been a gymnast for four years now, and she participates in local competitions. While she is quite good on the uneven bars, beam, and floor, she has struggled greatly with her vaults. On the first CD is the story of the little boy who was such a great hitter on his Little League team and how he accomplished this by "feeling" it.

Tee and I listened to this with great interest, then paused the CD to talk a bit about what Lynn had said, and whether it would be possible to apply this to her vaulting. We both agreed that it would be, and then we talked about how she could "feel it" and visualize it for 16 seconds. After our talk, she seemed pretty confident and told me that she was going to try using this technique. Later that night, after she came home from practice, I asked her if she had remembered to use the techniques. She replied, "Oh, yes!"

She went on to tell me that she was using it to feel her run, her feet going off the springboard, and her hands hitting on the vault itself. I asked her how it had worked. She was beaming. Her coach had said to her, "I don't know what clicked, but you have never looked better!" That was all she needed; she is now using this technique all the time.

She told me just today that she uses the "feelings place" many times throughout the day for a wide variety of things. She is also reminding me to get out of the grumpy place I go to and stop dwelling on what I don't want. Not too bad for an 11-year-old! I'm very excited for her. If I had learned this at such a young age, I can only imagine where my life would have taken me.

What about Tragedy?

Broken relationships, accidents, sickness, death . . . how do we apply the creation principles in these situations? Certainly, they are not easy to apply during times like these. But I thoroughly believe that if we apply the principles *all* the time, we can minimize the amount of tragedy we suffer.

Keep in mind, I am not here to tell people how to get over their own personal tragedies. I certainly don't want anyone else telling *me* how or when to "get over it." What I want to offer, when you are ready, is a way to apply these principles to help you move through these circumstances and get you back on your conscious creation path. The timing is yours and yours alone.

Any unexpected tragedy is bound to make you grab the bar tighter. It is really hard to put your attention on what you want when what you think you want has been suddenly taken away from you. The key here is to be easy on yourself, not to focus on the fact that you fell, but on the fact that you will eventually get up and get conscious again.

As you know, during the writing of this book, my partnership of seven years ended. I went through what we all go through in similar circumstances—denial, anger, grief, and, finally, letting go. At any point during this process I could have said, "Okay, I don't want to feel like this anymore, so I will simply put my attention on what I want and all will be fine." Fat chance. Believe me, I tried. I was just so heartbroken.

I went through the whole self-interrogation. "Where did it go wrong? What did I do wrong? How could I have let this happen?" It was a self-blame frenzy. All the while, I was aware that I wasn't applying the creation principles but, to be honest, I didn't care. Clearly, I wanted to feel my misery, and, boy, did I! I wanted to be a victim for a while, and so I was. My truth was my truth, and my experience was my experience. And you know what? What I experienced was all good! It was what I chose, so my life and I were still unfolding perfectly! I learned that:

- If I never experience being a victim, how can I know what being a creator really is?
- If I never experience grief, how can I know what joy really is?

- If I never experience pain, how can I know what pleasure really is?
- If I never experience trying to control everything, how can I know what the freedom of surrender can really mean for me?

If we are experiencing any of these things at any point, they must necessarily be a part of who we are. We are all of it, and the sooner we accept this as our truth, the sooner we can stop judging and learn to love and accept every part of ourselves. When we accept, we have choice. When we resist, we are bound to our judgments, and we can't choose that which we want to experience next.

How often do you judge what you are feeling? It seems crazy to be angry at yourself for being angry, but that's what I did. In doing so, I was perpetuating what I didn't want to be anymore. But it was still okay. The more I accepted myself and my feelings, the more I became the person I really wanted to be. It just took some time to figure it out.

During rough times, one of the questions we ask ourselves is, "Why did this happen to me?"

But, honestly, is it important to understand why it happened to you? Perhaps not. It's really important, however, to understand the intention behind the original question. Are you asking because you're curious and want to learn from this experience so that you can create your next experience? Or are you interested in blame?

In my case, I could easily see that I created my breakup unconsciously. I wasn't honest about my feelings, and while I didn't think I wanted the relationship to end, I certainly was not doing anything to help it survive.

For me, understanding my part in the breakup was important so that I could create my next ideal partnership from a foundation of honesty. It was worth answering the question "Why?" because it helped me to know who I wanted to be in my next relationship. Of course, this epiphany didn't come until after I indulged in the blame game for a while! But that's okay.

I think a lot of us use the question "Why?" to keep ourselves focused on whom to blame—a useless course of action. If we use this question instead to help us identify what we want next, it is a perfect use of our time because it helps to get us back on the path to getting our attention on what we want.

In the midst of loss, it can be really hard to think and feel our way out of it. Most of our thoughts and feelings are centered on our pain, and most of us have our attention on trying to figure out why this happened in the first place. Let's be clear: there is nothing wrong with our thoughts and feelings during these times! NOTHING. They are what they are. Allowing ourselves to experience them without judgment is the key to moving on and getting back on the creation course we want. It is important at these times to allow yourself to feel your feelings, to have compassion for yourself, and to honor how you feel right now. When you are ready to move past being the victim and back into your creator self, then you need to ask yourself:

- Is the focus of my attention right now getting me closer to what I want? Do my feelings support what I want?
- If I am analyzing why this happened, am I feeling what I want?
- If I am blaming myself and others, am I feeling what I want?
- If I am sad, am I feeling what I want?
- If I am resisting what is, am I feeling what I want?

The circumstances never change the principle. You attract what you think and feel.

I thank Idays for her story of triumph over tragedy:

It will be two years next Wednesday.
   I remember feeling confused about my life the weekend before it happened. I loved my son, Giovanni, very, very much, and I wanted the best for him, but I just didn't know what to do. Everywhere I looked, doors seemed to close in my face. The better job, the financial security, and the fulfilling family life I wanted just were not happening. I was depressed, broke, and experiencing problems in my marriage. I'd only been married for a month and a few weeks.

On Sunday, after I'd fed Giovanni and had my coffee, he fell asleep, and I picked up Lynn's book, *Excuse Me, Your Life Is Waiting*. I'd read it once before, and I remember asking myself what I was doing so wrong for my life to be headed in such an unwanted direction.

I continued to read for a while, and then I felt better.

That night, I gave Giovanni his milk before putting him to bed, and he slept on my stomach for a while, which he loved doing. At 1:00 A.M., I put him in his bassinet, and I slept in the little bed beside him. My husband came in and kissed him goodnight. Giovanni was due to wake up at 3:30 A.M. for his night feeding. I fell asleep.

I woke up again at 5:30 A.M., confused because Giovanni hadn't woken up to eat. I went to his bassinet and touched him and realized he was not breathing. I picked him up and ran to my husband. When he saw Giovanni, he jumped out of bed. I called 911. The operator walked my husband through CPR, and a few minutes later the cops and the ambulance arrived. They connected him to machines. I remember that the cop who was talking to me started to cry. I was very moved by his reaction; later I found out that he knew Giovanni was gone, and he didn't know how to tell me. Before we left for the hospital, my husband sat down on the floor and cried. Later, he told me that he already knew, too. When we arrived at the hospital, the doctor gave us the terrible news.

The days passed. After the burial, the pain grew stronger and stronger, and I felt I couldn't live without my baby. My husband tried to support me, but I interpreted his strength as a lack of love for Giovanni. I hated him for it, and I decided to leave our house. I hated everyone who gave me advice; I wondered if they would be able to take their own advice in my situation. Now I understand they were only trying to help.

A couple of months later, I found out that I was two months pregnant. I didn't know what to do. To be excited seemed unfaithful to my son's memory. My husband was happy when he heard the news, and he begged me to come home. I wasn't ready. For a long time, I could not forgive myself for not waking up to feed Giovanni. I figured that if I'd fed him at 2:30, I would have noticed what was going on and been able to save him somehow. The doctor said he died between 2:30 and 3:00. Still, I realized that blame was not going to bring my baby back.

After four months of separation, I decided to go back home. I started by reading Lynn's book from the beginning again. I'd blamed everything and everyone, including Lynn, because her principles didn't work, but later I realized her book was changing my life even as I was going through difficult times. Her principles were a great force and a great inspiration for me, and they helped me recuperate from my son's death. I started to absorb the positive from everything I was learning. One idea stuck to me like glue: I was NOT a victim, and I was the only one who could make my life better.

I also learned that the most important principle is love. I learned that hate, resentment, and grudges only make life bitter. I learned that I was playing the victim role without really noticing it, and I had been doing so all my life. I decided I didn't want to live the rest of my life that way. I wanted to feel more in control and to live in love. So that was my first step and the beginning of the most incredible journey of my life.

Little by little, I started realizing positive changes, first with my attitude toward others. I started appreciating my life. I started appreciating my family, and, most of all, I no longer felt guilty for loving and being happy for my pregnancy. I knew that my son, wherever he was, was happy for me. Maybe the reason he came into my life was to teach me how to find true happiness. I started to heal.

It was not a short process, though. And it's still ongoing. However, I am successfully mastering my feelings most of the time. I try to fill my days with happy thoughts and feelings, no matter how badly they begin.

The trick to overcoming my son's death was love. Yes, love. I felt love for all of the people who tried to help me and for everyone around me. I decided to feel love for this universe and to express it every day.

In the years before I had Giovanni, I had everything I needed to be happy, and yet I was not. I was always complaining. I never appreciated my luck. I had wonderful friends and family, but I never saw it. Now I notice the trees, the air. I find myself noticing these things now, and wondering why I never noticed them before. When I wake up in the morning with my husband and my daughter, I feel so grateful. I never take anything for granted anymore, not one single moment of happiness.

For times of tragedy, I offer a bit of encouragement: these principles will always be here for you. They will never leave you. When you are ready, simply choose to use them consciously, and they will continue to do their magic for you, just as they have always done. All you have to do is get conscious again!

What about My Health?

There are certain areas of our lives in which we feel we don't have much creative power, and one of these is definitely health. It has been pounded into our heads that we really don't have any control over our bodies—that we are victims of our bodies. But being the conscious creators that we are, we know that can't be true. In fact, we *do* have control over our bodies.

Creating health when our current circumstance involves sickness is not the easiest thing to do, but it can be done—and it has been done, by people just like us, who chose to put their attention on getting healthy again. It is not my intention to judge people's experiences when it comes to their health, but I do want to show you how to use creation principles to attain your desired health.

One of the first questions we usually ask ourselves when we get sick is, "Why did this happen to me?" or "Why am I sick?" I would invite you to ask another question: "Does my understanding of why I am sick help me to put my attention on being whole and healthy again?"

Circumstances change, but the principles don't. Where we place our attention, thoughts, and feelings is what we get. You can only be successful at restoring your health if your attention is placed solely on what you say you want. Remember, it is law.

So, if understanding why you got sick will help you get better—if it leads you, for example, to improve your diet or quit smoking—then focus on that, but then move forward on creating a "new you," not dwelling on the past. If getting sick was just a random event, then forget about understanding why you are sick and shift your attention right over to being whole and healthy again. Get a clear picture of what it would look and feel like to be restored to your healthy self.

I had an ailment once. For a long time, I concentrated on finding and rooting out the stress in my life that caused the pain. I was told the only cure would involve heavy sedation and a scalpel, and that just seemed like a little too much for me.

One day, I decided I was in perfect health, and therefore this issue was no longer part of my experience. I put my attention on what I wanted at a high level—to be healthy and happy. Putting attention on ridding myself of the ailment would have been a "don't want" in disguise. Every day, I reveled in my perfect health. As a result, I started making other healthy choices as well. One day, I noticed that I didn't need the medicine I had been using, and no longer had any more nasty symptoms. I still don't. For me, putting my attention on being healthy was a way to become healthy. And for Kristin, it was much the same.

When I was 14 years old, I went to see my doctor about some mild acne on my chest. He prescribed an antibiotic called tetracycline to help clear up my skin. Within 48 hours of being on the tetracycline, I was delirious.

In the school library doing research for an English assignment, I noticed the floor beneath me rocking, as if we were on a boat. My head was spinning, I could not focus, and it felt as if I were hovering a few inches above the gently swaying ground.

When the class bell rang, I walked to math in a half-lucid blur. I felt I existed in that half-lit moment of a dream when I'd just become aware of the fact that I was dreaming.

Halfway through math class, I knew that I had to go home. Fortunately, I lived only a few blocks away from my high school. Somehow, I walked home, and when I got to my bedroom, I was deliriously sure that if I wanted to fall asleep, I needed to lie on a 46-degree angle perpendicular to my bedpost, and my arms needed to form an equilateral triangle! Suffice it to say, we had just been reviewing geometry in class.

Although I felt better when I woke up, I still wasn't well. I was depressed, disoriented, and I felt as if things were not connecting properly in my mind. Even though I was convinced that the tetracycline—which I immediately stopped taking—was responsible for my state, I went back to see my doctor. He said there was nothing the medical community could do for someone with my symptoms; the only relevant medications might interfere with organ development and, thus, could not be given to a 14-year-old.

I tried to go on with my life as I had prior to taking the tetracycline, but I could not. I was so incredibly tired and confused. I became increasingly disoriented and started to experience difficulty understanding the simplest of concepts—a novel experience for an intelligent young woman.

My symptoms quickly escalated to the point were I did not feel comfortable leaving the house, let alone going to school. My friends kept calling to see what was wrong, but I didn't have any answers. I hated not having the answers.

Ashamed and embarrassed by an illness that I could not understand, I pushed my friends away and sank into a deep depression. I ignored all inquiries about the state of my health and tried to ignore what was happening to me.

I went through my own virtual hell. In addition to the depression, disorientation, and brain fog, I developed chronic anxiety and intense panic attacks. I remember lying in bed at night, rigid as a board, shaking. I would break out in cold sweats and try to stifle my terrified sobs so that I would not wake my family. My family, especially my mother, was very sympathetic to my plight, but I felt like such a failure and a burden. I willed myself to breathe in and out, in and out. With every breath—every single breath—I had to reassure myself that the anxiety would dissipate and that I would eventually be able to sleep. Some nights, when I was particularly afraid, I would write my mother detailed lists of my symptoms and leave them outside her bedroom door. That way, if she woke up to find me in a coma, my symptoms might provide her with a clue about what had happened to me.

I became disillusioned by Western, allopathic medicine. I was secretly terrified that I was merely a weak person and that my symptoms were all in my head, but still, I hoped that something might eventually help me, if only a little.

Over the course of the next six years, I pursued sequential homeopathy, acupuncture, energy work, yoga, meditation, lifestyle therapies, amino acid therapy, subliminal messaging tapes with active brain-wave therapy, and enzyme therapy, to name a few. I don't doubt that all of these contributed significantly to my recovery. However, no matter how much work I did, there was still something missing. Something was still standing in the way of a complete recovery. This missing link proved to be the life-transforming techniques set out by Lynn Grabhorn in her groundbreaking book, *Excuse Me, Your Life Is Waiting.* By working through *The* Excuse Me, Your Life Is Waiting *Playbook,* I learned how to be present to my own energy, without judgment or demand and without the need to fix or change anything. I learned how to accept myself as I am. In addition, I learned how to heal and transform my life by sinking into the energy of my desire. By embodying the energy, emotions, and experience of my heartfelt desires, I have transformed my life in ways more miraculous than I could ever have imagined.

Some people would have you believe that if you accept something, you are inviting it to stay. It really works the other way around: the more you put your attention on acceptance, the more your attention is off what you don't want. Now you have more time and energy to shift your attention onto things you do want!

When Kristin accepted her poor health, she was able to redirect all that energy into what she really wanted—great health. Then she was open to the thoughts and ideas that she felt would give her the health she really wanted!

So, accept your health exactly as it is and get clear on what you want to create next. Then trust yourself and your choices to allow your new experience of health to happen.

Has Anyone Made It through Lynn's "30 Days to Breakthrough" Program?

Lynn's program is nothing less than brilliant. Why? Because she invites you to put your powerful positive thoughts and feelings on the one thing that will make or break your conscious success with the principles of creation—YOU!

You will never be a master creator of your experience if you don't feel you deserve to be. It is impossible! Sure, you may get some results, but it will be hard to get consistent results. If deep down you don't feel that you deserve all that you can be, do, and have, you are not connected to your source and to your creation partner, and so you can't create what you want.

That is why she wanted us to focus on appreciating something—anything—about ourselves for 30 days. Unfortunately, most people I hear from can't make it through the first ten days! We just have never been encouraged before to appreciate ourselves. If anything, we've been encouraged to deny ourselves!

So, how do we get back to appreciating? Accept all that you are right now. Know that who you are right now is perfect. Choose to create something else if you want, but know that no matter what happens, you are pure goodness. Period.

This goes back to your new belief that I am not my current circumstance; I am the creator of it. I repeat . . .

- You are not a terrible person because you can't pay your bills.
- You are not a failure as a person if your business "fails."
- You are lovable even if your relationship ends.
- You are not less than whole because you are sick.

All these things are circumstances—they are not who you are. Who you are is the person who created these circumstances, and because you created them, you can choose to create a new set of circumstances. You have the power.

So now you have a choice: you can choose to personalize your circumstances and become this "terrible person," or you can choose to accept your circumstances and be the person who creates your new reality. Remember, either choice will be perfect, so don't beat yourself up if you choose to personalize. It is who you are right now, and who you are right now is always perfect, always!

Separating who you are from your circumstances is where your freedom to create yourself anew lies. Knowing that you are good, no matter what, allows your happiness to unfold!

People have asked how to "flip switch" when you just can't seem to. Remember the tools we discussed in chapter 4—understand your Victim MO, be your emotion, and switch focus. These tools will help you to master your 30 days.

For those of you who have tried Lynn's 30-day

program, understand that anytime you choose to be conscious, you are creating in a direction you want. Whether it is for 16 seconds or 30 days, you are making progress! So pat yourself on the back and always recognize any improvement in how you feel as success!

How Do I Implement These Principles When I Just Don't Believe They Will Work for Me?

Use these creation principles to create a new belief! As I have said before, these principles work on creating anything—including yourself and your beliefs!

Your "don't want" is—These principles won't work for me.

Your "do want" is—I am a master creator.

Typically, I would invite you to write your intention, script your end result, script who you are when you have what you want, and then think, speak, and act as the person who already has the experience you want.

This time, I'm going to ask you to flip the "think, speak, and act" part of this process. You've been told that your beliefs are hard to change. If you think they are, then that will be your experience. When you are having a tough time creating something, often it is help-ful to first *act* like the person who has the experience you really want. Forget about thinking and speaking first because you're having too much trouble with that.

Your belief starts as a thought. So if you want to cre-ate more money in your experience, but your belief is that you don't deserve it, then you will have a tough time thinking and speaking like someone who has a lot of money. But if you act *before* you think, thereby not allowing your thoughts to stop you, then you are allow-ing your creation partner a door to deliver what you have chosen to experience.

As you know, I wanted to experience more financial abundance in my life. I had a tough belief to overcome—that money doesn't come easily. If I wanted more money, to become the person who already had more money, I had to start acting that way.

One day, I was in a store, and they had a bucket for donations to victims of cancer. My first inclination was to donate, and then my thoughts kicked in. "Do I have enough money to give? Can I really afford to give away my money?" The person who was experiencing financial abundance wouldn't have thought twice about it, so I decided to act like that person. I stuck my hand in my pocket, and the smallest bill I had was a ten.

Again, I had reticent thoughts. "Isn't that a bit much?" And again I reminded myself that this was a no-brainer for someone who was experiencing financial abundance, so I acted like one and threw in the ten-dollar bill.

Did I run out of money? On the contrary, when I got home I had two e-mails requesting my coaching, a current client said she was going to sign on for another month, and I got my tax return from my accountant announcing that I was getting over $3,000 back.

Now, did all this abundance come because I chose to act like a person experiencing financial abundance? You bet it did!

Rebecca had a similar experience . . .

Rebecca wanted to buy a house. Not only did she want to buy a house, but she wanted to buy one in one of the most expensive suburbs of Boston. Rebecca and her partner already owned a summer house and a condo, which was used as a studio for her partner's work as a photographer. Rebecca felt great about her intention for a new house, but she was struggling with the fact that having three houses felt somewhat wasteful. More important, she felt she didn't deserve to have so much when so many other people didn't even have roofs over their heads.

Rebecca's belief was preventing her from being the person who already owned her ideal home. She couldn't possibly think, speak, and act like the person because her primary thought was that she didn't deserve so much abundance.

Rebecca became aware that she needed to change her belief if she was going to attract her ideal home, so she started acting like the person she imagined would deserve her ideal home—a person who gives back to society. She started volunteering at the Boston Food Bank, and last I heard, she's even launching a musical program called Kids Café that sponsors professional musicians to come in and play for kids while they eat lunch.

She kept her attention on noticing all of the abundance in her life, and she started being grateful, not resentful, when unanticipated expenses came up. She was grateful for all of her experiences, even the perceived "bad" ones. She started acting worthy of everything that came into her experience.

By putting her attention on acting like someone who is worthy of owning three homes, Rebecca is now able to use positive words and have positive thoughts about her worthiness. She is creating a powerful new belief that she is worthy of all the abundance she really wants!

So how do you become a master creator? Start acting like one! Consciously use these principles, act like they are working, and they will work. Take credit for your experience and choose to create another one if you want. Act like the person who loves this process and uses it consciously, and you will be that person!

And my all-time favorite question . . .

How Do I Let Go and *Be* All This without Looking Like a Crazy Person?

I love this question. We've been *being* something we are not for so long—a grumbling whiner, an ungrateful plodder, a quiet victim, or some other unhappily distant version of ourselves—so wouldn't we expect people to look at us, mouths agape, when all of a sudden we are calm, peaceful, and joyful?

Rest easy, this a calm process. You won't become a different person; you'll just shed those actions and qualities that are not in alignment with the real you, and amplify those parts of you that are you. By the way, your friends and family will probably thank you for letting go of some of your less savory characteristics, which probably weren't all that pleasant to be around anyway!

Ever notice how people are attracted to the person in the room who seems the most authentic? There is an important reason for that. Deep down inside, we all want to be that person. We all want to be the person we really are, no holds barred. We all crave to live our truth. Why else do you think you are reading this book?

Now, some grouchy people may mutter that you've changed or that you're not being yourself. They might object to your dreamy joy, your spontaneous jigs, or your newfound ability to find beauty around you. I invite you to take their objections as a good indication that you are headed in the right direction, as long as the changes feel good to you.

Also, take comfort in the fact that you don't have to evangelize these principles. You don't have to amass converts, make cold calls, or hold bake sales. Just live with them in your own silence, and you will start to attract like-minded people.

We all desire to be who we really are. By becoming who *you* are and, in turn, having all that you want, you are naturally inspiring those around you to reach for the same.

If people think you are crazy for being authentic, then being crazy is a good thing. Enjoy it! Do that jig if you want to.

Creation Principles Really Work!

Hillary wanted out of her current living situation. She wanted her own apartment, but she wasn't sure how she could afford it. She set an intention to be out of her apartment and into a new one by August of that year. In July, her friend asked her if she wanted to move in with her until she found a place. Hillary still wanted to live alone, but considering her situation, this was a great opportunity. She packed up all her stuff and hopped into her friend's car. As they were driving, Hillary's friend got a call. Someone she knew was going to be gone for several months and wanted to know if she knew anyone who needed an apartment, rent-free, if they would agree to take care of her cats!

Now, you would think that this was the answer Hillary was looking for, but when she really put her feelings into it, she decided that staying with her friend was what she wanted to do. She lived with her friend, had a lot of fun, and, of course, found the apartment she had been scripting. She moved in August 1!

SEVEN

My Intention for You . . . Right NOW

You deserve it all. You deserve to have all of
your aspirations realized, no matter what
they may be. That is a cosmic guarantee.

—Lynn Grabhorn,
Excuse Me, Your Life Is Waiting

I started this book with the story of how I created,
or semiconsciously created, the book deal. I thought I
would end it with a demonstration of how I consciously
created the actual book. I'd never written a book before,
so I realized I'd better get conscious . . . and fast!

So, my intention was: "*Excuse Me, Your Life Is
NOW* is the perfect follow-up book to *Excuse Me, Your
Life Is Waiting* because it teaches readers, through real-
life examples, how to practically and consistently apply
the creation principles so that they can enjoy their lives
right now! It is a simple, powerful, inspiring, and practical book."

My intention led me to the following script: "The
process of writing *Excuse Me, Your Life Is NOW* is easy,
natural, effortless, fun, and quick. The thoughts and
words pour out of me. I am constantly connected to my

creation partner while writing, and I know that what I am writing is perfect for everyone who picks up the book. I find a comfortable way of writing and am amazed at how simple the process really is. I am constantly guided and open to all the new ideas and thoughts that pour in and feel great. I love writing this book!"

So what was the downside of me writing this book?

- I would be wide open to criticism.
- I had never written a book before.
- I would have to spend a lot of time away from my family.
- My business might suffer while I was writing it.
- I might not be able to handle the business the book might generate.

Who knew I could have so many hidden "don't wants"? I needed to get to work on clearing these fast.

My "do wants":

- I am grateful for all the feedback that makes my book even more valuable to my readers.
- I am excited to learn about the book-writing process.
- I successfully balance my time between my family, business, and the writing of this book.
- I have everything I need in place to welcome clients generated by this book.

So my new script became: "The process of writing *Excuse Me, Your Life Is NOW* is easy, natural, effortless, fun, and quick. The thoughts and words pour out of me. I am constantly connected to my creation partner while writing, and I know that what I am writing is perfect for everyone who picks up the book. I find a comfortable way of writing and am amazed at how simple the process really is. I am constantly guided and open to all the new ideas and thoughts that pour in and feel great. All the feedback I get makes the book even more powerful, and I love learning about the book-writing process. I love that my family, business, and the writing of this book are all perfectly balanced. I welcome all the new business this book will generate for me! I love writing this book, and am so grateful for this opportunity!"

Much better! Now, who was I going to be? I had to get clear on what my thoughts, words, and actions were going to be for the next several months.

Thoughts:

My thoughts and feelings were centered on being the author of *Excuse Me, Your Life Is NOW*, and loving the fact that writing was such an effortless process!

Words:

I was conscious to use only positive words when it came to answering questions about how my writing was going.

Actions:

My actions were to always trust and let the process unfold naturally—no forcing allowed!

The whole process started in February 2006. The first thing that needed to be done was to get some real-life examples. My publisher put announcements on all its Web sites and on Lynn's, too. At first, we weren't getting many replies. In the past, I would have been anxious, but instead I chose to put my attention on the fact that my creation partner delivers what I choose for myself without fail. Then I had an idea: my creation partner works through me! I jumped on Amazon and read the reviews. Then I contacted the folks who wrote the reviews to see if they would like to submit a story. After that, the stories started pouring in!

Then my relationship ended. Let's just say that during this time I wasn't feeling like doing much of anything. I allowed myself to take the time and feel what I needed to feel. I chose to trust that everything was unfolding perfectly, including me and the book!

I decided that I would start writing in June, pull it all together in July, and then edit in August. I started with a brain dump, just writing everything that came to mind that I wanted to share with my readers. When I would get tense about the fact that I really didn't have a format yet, I would remind myself that my intention was already complete: I had written a simple, powerful, inspiring, and practical book—it was already done—so I must have come up with a format at some point!

When I told people what I was doing, they were very excited for me, but they would say, "Writing a book is such a huge job" or "It must be so hard to write a book." During these times, I would thank them and say that it wasn't really all that hard. In fact, it seemed pretty effortless! This was around the same time that an opportunity to work with an editor came into my experience, without my asking for it, someone who had read and loved *Excuse Me, Your Life Is Waiting*!

And then came July, when I didn't write a word! In July, I felt like reading more, so I did. I felt like doing some inner exploration, so I did. I decided that it was important for me to "be," and then to "do"—and so I did. In the past, I would have been going out of my mind, terrified because my book was due in two months, and here I was doing everything but writing. But it just felt right; I had intended to allow my creation partner to deliver this book through me, so my job was to make sure that I kept doing what felt right. In July, what felt right was not writing! What I realized also during this time was that time really didn't matter. The book was already done in my intention, so it would be finished whether I wrote in July or not!

I also learned one more important thing in July. If I didn't finish the book, or even if I finished the book and my publisher thought it was junk, or even if I had to return the first part of my advance, or even if I lost all my credibility, I would still be fine because I am not my circumstance; I am its creator. I was able to surrender to the fact that if the opposite of what I had intended were to happen, I would still be okay. When I did surrender, I was able to release all the energy consumed by any doubt, fear, or worry, and allow it to be used for the flow of my creation process. That's when things really broke open!

In August, my writing resumed, but it was much different from when I wrote back in June. It was clear, and it was coming more from my heart. The time I took in July to just "be" helped me to be more comfortable with who I was and what I wanted to write. Writing felt much better, and I know this book is much better for it! It seemed that just the right stories would come at just the right time. Of course, there were also those times where I started to panic, especially when it came to the number of pages. I think this goes back to my school days when my essays had to be a certain number of words. All I know is that I started to worry about page numbers and not about what I wanted to say. I talked to four people about my fears, and every single one of them said that it was my job to make sure that I was saying all that I wanted to say, and that the pages would take care of themselves. I knew my creation partner was giving me the message I wanted to hear through my friends! So, I continued writing, and enjoying the process, too!

I know that this book is what I intended it to be because I trusted myself and allowed it to come through me naturally. The process was easy, natural, effortless, fun, and quick! Sure, there were times when I almost slipped into the "tortured writer's spiral"—especially when I bumped a huge cup of iced tea, and it spilled all over my keyboard, or when I accidentally deleted this section and had to rewrite it from scratch. But through it all, I kept my attention on the fact that the book was already written and that everything was unfolding perfectly, and so it did!

Believe it or not, I don't consider this book to be my reward. I consider my true reward to be the fact that I was able to consciously create the book! I love the fact that during this process I became the person who could use my power to consciously create. The way I feel about my ability to implement the laws and the creation process will serve me in every area of my life. And they will serve you, too!

Now you, too, have the inspiration and the tools to create the life experience you really want. I leave you with some intentions of my own. My powerful, positive intention for you is that you allow yourself to be:

- open and receptive to all that your creation partner has and is providing for you.
- grateful for all of your creations—the great and the not-so-great—for they will guide you to understand what you want to create next.
- connected through your powerful positive thoughts and feelings with who you really are and with your powerful creator.
- the creator you are with all your heart and mind.
- focused and centered on what you have chosen to create.
- the person who sees the world as you choose to see it.
- the person today who has what you have chosen for tomorrow.
- the person who chooses to move beyond fear, doubt, and worry to love and creation.
- what you really are: a joyful, loving, accepting, blessing, and grateful person. May you be all these things so that you can and will enjoy your life RIGHT NOW!

And, finally, a message straight from Lynn. She wrote it to one of her readers, but I believe that she would say it to all of us if she were still around.

Keep it up, and don't beat yourself up if your silver spoon seems to tarnish now and then. Get out your polish, and start again.
All the best,
Lynn G.

So, If Lynn Was Using Creation Principles, Why Did She Die?

Truth is, I don't know, and it's important that we accept that we can't know what anyone other than ourselves is creating. Lynn is the only expert and creator of her experience, as are you in your own, and I believe that is the message she sent us in a letter she posted on her Web site shortly before her death:

To all my friends, family, and the rest of you wonderful guys . . .

My work here on this planet is done, and I've now joined others of the Light in a higher dimension to help facilitate the forthcoming "Birth" that this planet and universe is about to experience.

Please. PLEASE! If you have to grieve for me, hold it down to a couple of minutes, and then be done with it, for that kind of energy placed on one who has just "left" can be torturous.

Frankly, I'm excited about where I'm going, and what's coming down for all of us. Yes, both hard times and great times are coming, but I beg you, STAY with the principles of *Excuse Me*. Teach those principles in seminars, workshops, books, speaking engagements, and one-on-one. That is more important than I could ever put into words.

Let people know of the steps in *Dear God . . .* , so critically important to every individual. And then get them into the fun and excitement of *Planet Two.* Teach! Spread the word! Make it UN-woo-woo, and totally down to earth.

You're a hearty, determined bunch, and while I may not know you in human person, I love you so very much. Don't stop . . . don't stop . . . DON'T STOP!!!!!!!!! You're going to be a part of an amazing new world and universe that is almost finished.

My deepest love to you all,
Lynn Grabhorn

Acknowledgments

To Lynn Grabhorn: without your profound and simple work, I would never have had this amazing opportunity. I know you had your hand in this from the get-go, and I thank you for inspiring me through the process. My deepest thanks for your work and inspiration!

To all of you who sent me your stories and were kind enough to take the time to speak with me. I enjoyed being with each and every one of you and am so grateful for your desire to share your experiences in an effort to keep Lynn's work alive. My deepest gratitude to those of you whose stories were selected for this book: Kim, Julia, Lisa, Vivian, Christina, Carolyn N., Denise, William, Jeff, Robert, Susan, Jan, Carolyn F., Connie, Olivia, Raechel, Michele, Jane, Rebecca, Nan, Tee, Kristin, Sherri, Jay, Sebastian, Hillary, and especially Idays. Thank you for your courage to inspire others!

To all of my clients, past and present: through our work together, you have taught me so much about myself—at times I really think I should be paying you! Thank you for making my dreams come true by allowing me to play a little part in the making of yours.

To Lisa Brennan-Jobs, my first editor, thank you for being with me down to the wire and for giving me that extra support when I chose to let a bit of doubt creep in. You have been a great writing partner in one of the greatest experiences of my life! To Susan Heim, my second editor, thank you for your thoughts, know-how, and wisdom.

To Bob Friedman and Jack Jennings for taking a chance on me. Jack, in honor of you, I have used the word "manifest" very sparingly! Bob, thank you not only for this opportunity, but for introducing me to the works of Neale Donald Walsch. You must have known intuitively that I was ready for it.

To my mom, Irene Meehan, for loving me by making a conscious effort to allow me my own experience. To Amy O'Neil for being my friendship soul mate, always there without judgment through thick and thin. To Susan Wagner and Shannon Knight, for always being there for me, especially when I needed you the most over this past year. To Susan Wilson and Rebecca Strauss, for our new friendship that continues to grow. To Nancy and Billy Fabbri, your kindness is surpassed only by your generosity. Thank you for all you have done for me and all that you continue to do for Sammi. To Terri Bessette, for teaching me what it means to be a great parent and for your support with Sammi during the writing of this book! To Rebecca, Joseph, Matty, and Steven Valeri, thank you for playing with Sammi so that I could take the much-needed time to write. To my Starbucks buddies, Seth Bond and Ron Thimot, thank you for reminding me to KISS (keep it simple, stupid).

To my nieces and nephew, Jordan, Hannah, and Zyon Bessette. You have been my greatest teachers since I first met you seven years ago. It has been an honor to be such a big part of your lives!

To my daughter, Samantha Jake Banaszak-Fabbri, thank you for constantly reminding me who I really am and what I am really capable of. In your eyes, I see that I will always be loved unconditionally!

To two people who have been particular inspirations while writing this book—Alanis Morrisette and Neale Donald Walsch. Alanis, I never thought "You Oughta Know" would apply to me; I didn't know how much "That I Would Be Good" would save me; and I now truly understand how "Thank You" will keep me going. Thank you for your unabashed sharing of your journey. I have been inspired by it and you for years! And Neale, when Bob Friedman and I were having dinner, he asked if I had read your book, *Conversations with God*. I promptly said no because I thought it would be about religion. He let me know that that was not the case and recommended I pick it up anyway, and so I did. Like people have said of Lynn's work, I have read it over and over again. *Conversations* was literally a godsend when "who I really am" was up in the air during a personally volatile year. Thank you for all that you have done and continue to do!

To everyone whose books I've read, and words I've heard on the topic of discovering our power, thank you for your inspiration. I'm sure you will recognize little pieces of yourself in this work. Thank you also to Esther and Jerry Hicks, who inspired Lynn to write *Excuse Me*. Without the Hicks' work, we may never have been introduced to Lynn and her unique perspective on how to apply the creation principles!

Your Daily Conscious Creation Program in a Nutshell

It is almost time to put down this book and implement your own creation program. Are you ready?

If you walk away with just one point from this book, it's that by being and doing what feels good, you attract all that you want. You are the only expert in what feels good to you, so my giving you a 12-step program is not in your best interest. But here's your chance to put the principles to the test by creating a Daily Conscious Creation Program that feels good to you!

This is the "how-to" part of the book, but remember, you are going to create the "how-to" that works for you. I have pulled out the important points for you to consider as part of your program. I invite you to go back to each section and see what really resonates with you and then apply it. If you feel that you already have an area down pat, then move on. This is your program, so *you* choose what to put your attention on.

By now you know the drill all too well:

List your "don't wants":

_____

_____

_____

_____

_____

_____

Turn your "don't wants" into "do wants":

_____

_____

_____

_____

_____

_____

Then, write your intention script—the end result you want—for your Daily Conscious Creation Program.

_____

_____

_____

_____

_____

_____

_____

Write your being script—the feelings you are being—for your Daily Conscious Creation Program.

_____

_____

_____

_____

_____

_____

Some Common Techniques

What we are really doing here is transforming who you are by how you think and feel. What you think about is what starts the ball rolling, so this program is all about filling your mind with powerful, positive thoughts. When your thoughts are positive, your feelings become positive. With that said, here are a couple of techniques that can help to raise your consciousness about what you're thinking and feeling:

Affirmations—These are short, powerful phrases that, when stated, help to shift your thinking. The Creation Foundation Beliefs are, in essence, affirmations. Saying them, with feeling and out loud, can really help to bring them to mind when you are feeling less than conscious. Coming up with your own is also powerful. For me, the affirmation, "Money and clients are pouring into my experience effortlessly," comes in handy when I allow a bit of fear about my business to sneak into my thoughts. Affirmations are anything that you want to believe. So create some and see how quickly they replace your unwanted thoughts in just a short period of time.

Visualization—This is when you can actually see and

feel yourself as the person who is already enjoying what you want. Please don't worry if you can't actually "see" yourself; it is more important that you feel the feelings. It's as easy as closing your eyes and putting your attention on being the person who already has what you want.

Meditation—This offers you an opportunity to just be. It involves quieting the mind and allowing yourself to be calm and peaceful. It's an opportunity to know that in this moment everything is perfect.

Gratitude—Writing down what you're grateful for is a powerful way to demonstrate that you are the person who already has what you want. Writing it down is great, but BEING it is even better! Think about what you are grateful for throughout your day and say "thank you."

I will mention some books on these techniques in the resources section that follows. Again, look into the ones that resonate with you, not the ones you think you should do.

There are two parts to your program: the doing part and the being part.

1. *The Doing Part of Your Program*—This is where you take the time to sit and consciously work on your intentions and your scripts. It is also the time that you will want to do your visualizations and affirmations if you choose.

2. *The Being Part of Your Program*—This is where you put conscious attention on who you are being throughout your day. Remember, being conscious is a full-time job!

So, let's step through the book and pull out all of the elements that will help you to develop your program!

Getting Started

This is where you get clear on what you intend so that you can begin to be conscious of it on a daily basis.

- Review the laws.
- Affirm the seven Creation Foundation Beliefs.
- Write your intentions. If you are stuck in not knowing what you want, then go to page 43 for more help in this area. You can create as many intentions as you feel are manageable.
- Write your intention script for this area.
- Identify any resistance.
- Remember that you already have what you want.
- Create your being script.
- Choose your thoughts, words, and actions.
- Review the obstacles.

Daily Doing

This is where you start thinking about how you want to create your program. You might want to consider incorporating the following:

- Affirm, out loud, the seven Creation Foundation Beliefs.
- Write what you are grateful for.
- Review your intentions and scripts. Say them out loud, with feeling. If you don't feel them, then change them!
- Visualize your scripts, and see and feel yourself being the person who already has what you want. Simply run through each of your scripts, making sure that you see and feel the end result that you want.
- Take a moment to just be, knowing that this moment and every next moment is perfect now that you have chosen to be a conscious creator.

- Take a moment to commit to only thinking, speaking, and acting in alignment with what you have chosen.

Daily Being

Be conscious throughout your day that you are the person who already has what you want. Pay attention to your thoughts, words, and actions. Be and feel the feelings of the person who already has what you ultimately want. Know that because you have done your job, your creation partner is delivering all that you have chosen to experience to you. Be in the moment, and keep your positive thoughts and feelings flowing.

When You Experience Creation Frustration

Do not waste energy beating yourself up! Simply acknowledge that you are frustrated and choose to switch your attention!

- Review "Switching Focus," page 94.
- Review chapter 6.

Never fear, you only have to become conscious so that you can remember who you are and how life really works. Most of us don't remember because it was socialized out of us starting when we were kids. Once you become conscious for a while, creating will become as natural as breathing again.

There you have it—all the information and tools at your disposal to start enjoying your roller-coaster ride! So, throw your hands up in the air and always remember: your creation partner is right next to you, ready to deliver what you choose when you are willing to allow it.

Resources for Conscious Creators

Who's the expert? YOU! Our first inclination when we get inspired is to run off and find out everything we can on a particular topic. Then what happens? We end up learning about other cool topics, and we start seeking out more information about them, too. In the end, we never apply anything because we are too busy gaining knowledge.

I suggest you set up your Daily Conscious Creation Program and then look to these additional resources to supplement it. Always keep in mind that seeking is not creating!

With that said, here are some great Web sites to keep you inspired and to deepen your understanding. Some I have used personally, and others have been recommended by readers of *Excuse Me, Your Life Is Waiting.*

www.excusemeyourlifeisnow.com—For more information, coaching, and seminars.

www.excusemecourse.com—For Lynn's on-line course.

www.nealedonaldwalsch.com—For all of Neale's books and the "Conversations with God" trilogy.

www.alanis.com—For music with inspiring lyrics.

www.OpenFlame.biz—Sometimes a physical experience can help you to break through your fear. A fire walk is an amazing experience that can help you do just that. When we believe it, we can achieve it. Stop living a life of fear. Start living a life of freedom!

www.PositiveFeelingsRule.com—A site to help college students learn to live the life they want.

www.TheSecret.tv—A powerful movie on the Law of Attraction.

www.WhattheBleep.com—Another powerful movie on our power to create.

www.abraham-hicks.com—Lynn credits the teachings of Abraham for inspiring some of the principles in *Excuse Me, Your Life Is Waiting*. The work of Esther and Jerry Hicks can really help to keep you on track!

www.Monday9am.tv—Truly inspiring videos that support the concepts you are learning to live!

www.tut.com—Register for Mike's "Notes from the Universe." They are funny, inspiring, and most often dead-on with what we need to help us to keep our attention on what we want!

www.journey-to-success.com—This is a great site with complementary philosophies. Jessica, who runs it, is a great person who gets the concepts of manifestation and creation!

www.SabianSymbols.com—Since I believe we are all creators, I don't usually recommend getting astrology readings, but I do want to recommend Lynda and her work. I did the reading to see if it was on track with what I was intending to create and it was! In addition, it helped me to identify some emotions I was dealing with, which helped me to move through them faster.

www.ecstaticrelations.com—Carolyn North's book, *Ecstatic*

Relations, is about the invisible love glue that holds the universe together, the ecstatic longing and attraction we feel toward a person with whom we have fallen in love. It presents six true stories from the life of a woman who loves frequently and well, and brief commentaries on the universal metaphor that each story represents.

BONUS CHAPTER

What I've Learned Since Writing
Excuse Me, Your Life Is NOW

There's always something more to learn about the Law of Attraction and creation principles. Visit www.excusemeyourlifeisnow.com to download your bonus chapter of *Excuse Me, Your Life Is NOW*. This chapter introduces you to even more advanced strategies that I have learned since writing this book. You will learn:

- About the power of "willingness"
- More on moving beyond judgment
- How to manage your perception
- How you can create even more by doing even less

Find out more at www.excusemeyourlifeisnow.com.

About the Author

Doreen Banaszak is a teacher, author, and coach who left a 15-year corporate career to create the life and business she really wanted. Through her teaching, writing, and coaching, she has been instrumental in helping hundreds of people create the lives they really want, not the lives they think they should have. Doreen offers one-on-one coaching as well as group presentations on mastering the Law of Attraction. Find out more at www.excusemeyourlifeisnow.com.

HAMPTON ROADS
PUBLISHING COMPANY, INC.

Thank you for reading *Excuse Me, Your Life Is Now,* the newest book in a new *Excuse Me* series that applies the successful Law of Attraction principle to specific aspects of our daily lives. In 2000 Hampton Roads published Lynn Grabhorn's *Excuse Me, Your Life Is Waiting,* which became a *New York Times* bestseller. Hundreds of thousands of readers have felt their lives transformed by Lynn's message. Lynn's book has brought us positive energy that has attracted other authors whose lives are guided by the principles she espoused.

Excuse Me, Your Life Is Waiting
The Astonishing Power of Feelings
Lynn Grabhorn

Ready to get what you want? Half a million readers have answered with an enthusiastic "yes" and have embraced Lynn's principles for achieving the life of their dreams. This upbeat yet down-to-earth book reveals how our true feelings work to "magnetize" and create the reality we experience. Part coach, part cheerleader, Lynn lays out the nuts and bolts of harnessing the raw power of your feelings. Once you become aware of what you're feeling, you'll turn the negatives into positives and literally draw all those good things to you like a magnet, creating the life you know you were meant to have—right now!

Discover the secrets that have made *Excuse Me* a *New York Times* bestseller!

Paperback • 328 pages • ISBN 978-1-57174-381-7 • $16.95

www.hrpub.com   1-800-766-8009

The Excuse Me, Your Life Is Waiting *Playbook*
With the Twelve Tenets of Empowerment
Lynn Grabhorn

Human beings have evolved physically, socially, and technologically, but are unable to take the next step toward spiritual evolution because of self-defeating habits and conditioning—in short, we are our own victims. Lynn Grabhorn has taken the concepts that made *Excuse Me, Your Life Is Waiting* a bestseller and transformed them into a complete workbook for empowerment. The clearly focused explanations, discussion material, meditations, and exercises are essential building blocks to a new way of being.

Trade paper • 288 pages • ISBN 978-1-57174-270-4 • $22.95

Excuse Me, Your Job Is Waiting
Attract the Work You Want
Laura George

New York Times bestselling author Lynn Grabhorn showed half a million readers how to "magnetize" their emotions to draw their desires to them. Now, human resource manager Laura George applies Grabhorn's powerful Law of Attraction to the life experiences of both losing and getting a job. George captures the style and substance of *Excuse Me* and helps you identify the qualities you want in a job and then shows you how to flip the negative feelings you may be carrying ("the economy is terrible"; "I can't believe I got laid off"; "I'm too old") so you can stay focused and upbeat to draw that perfect job to you.

Paperback • ISBN 978-1-57174-529-3 • 312 pages • $16.95

Hampton Roads Publishing Company

. . . for the evolving human spirit

HAMPTON ROADS PUBLISHING COMPANY publishes books
on a variety of subjects, including metaphysics, spirituality,
health, visionary fiction, and other related topics.

For a copy of our latest trade catalog, call toll-free,
800-766-8009, or send your name and address to:

HAMPTON ROADS PUBLISHING COMPANY, INC.
1125 STONEY RIDGE ROAD • CHARLOTTESVILLE, VA 22902
e-mail: hrpc@hrpub.com • www.hrpub.com